The Inpatient Years

TO MY HUSBAND, BILL

Jean Kaiserling

Quantum Discovery
A LITERARY AGENCY

Library of Congress Control Number: 2024926201

ISBN
979-8-89641-011-9 (Paperback)
979-8-89641-012-6 (eBook)

Introduction

After my husband died, I fell deeper and deeper into grief. My psychiatrist called it "stuck in grief." And with that came more and more reasons to not take care of myself. My goal was to die. But there was still something that kept me hanging on to life. Every time I grew closer to death, psychiatrist and therapists advised me to go into the psychiatric hospital to lessen the crisis I was in. Sometimes I would agree with them, and sometimes I would fight it for a few weeks. But inevitably I would end up in "intake" to stay a week or so.

This book describes my routine in and out of this hospital during my many times there. Included is a lot of sadness since Bill died, but I have included some of the happy times of our life together.

It's hard to tell just where this life will take me. Some days I'm extremely depressed, but at other times I get involved in some sort of project that gives me a brief respite from this grief. I also recently got a new dog, Nisha, to follow in the very sad death of my lovely last dog, Lady. Nisha is a sweet dog and shares her love with me, which is of great help.

I'm hoping this book helps others with the life-changing events that can occur when we lose a loved one. Whether you lose a husband, a wife, a child, or even a pet, loss creates a huge change that can affect our entire lives.

Welcome to my journey...

~Jean Kaiserling

*Almighty Father—please help me. I pray every
day, but I need your guidance. I have so many
requests of you. I still haven't learned to slow
down and listen for what you want of me.
What you want of my life now. My purpose.*

I spend a lot of time suffering, crying, and knowing I've gone through almost three lonely years since I lost the love of my life—Bill. My husband of twenty-four years, taken from me because of a horrible work accident that caused hot, compressed steam to burn most of his body.

Days of hope and fear mixed together in the hospital. And then, devastation. Bill, only fifty-eight years old, gone after nineteen agonizing days. Our wonderful life together turned upside down.

I remember those events over and over. They are the last I have of Bill. Happy memories that don't help because they lead directly back to the sad memories. Every day, feeling the loss of Bill is devastating. I keep remembering a dream I had a few weeks after I lost Bill. I was sleeping and I was reliving the ringing of the phone—when Bill's work partner called to tell me Bill had been burnt. I answered the phone in my thoughts. It was Bill, telling me, "I won't be coming home." I awoke with a startle. It all felt so real. *Was it really Bill trying to help me accept what had happened?* I wondered. I haven't learned to accept it yet.

This long winter and being alone have been getting to me. Time is passing without my paying much attention to it. I sit in my living room, staring out the window at nothing but snow. I'm going through a particularly tough time again. I'm constantly feeling numb, strongly feeling I can't continue suffering the loss of Bill. I ponder desperately, *What else can I do?*

My rock has been God. When I can pray deeply and privately to God, I feel his comfort. But at times, I think my grief and depression block God's comfort from me. I become numb, speechless, thoughtless. And then I feel desperate.

I crave isolation so I can think about Bill as often as I want. I can also choose if I want to stay quiet, if I want to cry, if I want to pray, or if I want to stare at the wall, without trying to interact with someone else. But I'm being told by friends, family—and my psychiatrist—that I should plan an activity away from my house every day. That is difficult. Most socializing doesn't come easy for me anymore. I'd rather be helping someone who needs help. So I guess it's good that I have an ongoing project at the home of my brother, Roger.

We—my long-time helper and Bill's long-time best friend, Dave; Tommy, Dave's nephew; and Tom, Dave's brother-in-law—have been working at Roger's house for some time. We painted his garage and the trim on his house, and Dave and I are now working inside.

It's important for me to help Roger right now. Both Roger and Dave were laid off from their companies. Luckily both of their wives are still working, but the timing was lousy for Roger, because while he was still working, he had a contractor put an addition on his house. The outside was done, but the inside was not, and we had planned to do the rest of the inside work ourselves. The electrical work, the insulation, and the drywall are finally complete, so now we need to finish the mudding, the painting, the woodwork—and on and on.

Unfortunately, mudding is my job. Mudding is putting joint compound into the cracks of the drywall and spreading it out thin so the seams don't show. I learned to mud while working on a bathroom at my house. Sadly, I'm good at it, so it's my job. But it seems like even more work now, because I've developed aches and pains, especially when trying to mud the ceiling. I went to a doctor and he diagnosed me with fibromyalgia. I take a medication for it, but it still hurts, so I'm pretty much stuck with the pain.

I've always enjoyed Dave as a friend. Bill introduced Dave and Jaci to me long ago, and the four of us have enjoyed getting together when we could. Dave does a good job of understanding my pain of losing Bill, which is comforting to me.

Now I would like to find a group with similar experiences and understanding of this kind of loss. I started checking lists of "help" groups, but I haven't found anything that matches me so far. Shortly after Bill died, I tried a grief group, but it didn't feel right to me. So, sadly, I quit.

April 2012

During the winter my older dog, Deogee, a black Labrador, was starting to have trouble getting up and walking in the snow. I would put a harness on her and try to help her walk by lifting her back end. I knew the time was coming when I would have to do something about it. She was fifteen years old—quite old for a big dog. She was still quite happy, but I wasn't sure how much pain she was in. She developed a routine: when she couldn't get up off the floor, she would bark gently at me, and I would help lift her back end up. By the time I got her up, her tail would be wagging while she walked in circles—a cute sight.

But now it was becoming too difficult for her. She was scared to go outside, and she was having quite a few accidents.

I couldn't bear to think about what I was going to have to do, but I didn't want her to suffer anymore.

I called Roger to see if he would go to the veterinarian with me. I knew he would because he's such an animal lover. I wasn't able to lift Deogee into the car, so I sat in the back and Roger put her in my lap.

The ride to the vet was horribly sad, although Deogee actually looked happy sitting in my lap. I was trying not to cry because I didn't want her worrying about me.

At the vet's office, I held her while they gave her the drug. In a few minutes, her body became lifeless. I was devastated— she had been such a wonderful dog.

Roger and I were both crying as we drove home. I had already held three other dogs of mine when it was their time. It never gets easier. I hope all of my dogs will be waiting for me when I get to Heaven. I told myself, *Bill is with them now.*

May 2012

As soon as May appeared, my thoughts again quickly turned to the anniversary of the day Bill and I met, May 28, 1982—the Friday of Memorial Day weekend. Even though the anniversary wasn't until the end of the month, memories were already floating in my head. These memories are bittersweet because they give me a split second of happiness, followed by the heartache of facing the loss of Bill.

During these times—which are often—I keep deep in isolation, not wanting anything to change my suffering. Somehow I feel closer to Bill the more I suffer. Bill would hate this, and I don't really understand it. So I continue to see my psychiatrist, Dr. John, and my therapists, hoping their counsel and the medications I am on will somehow help me. And, against medical advice, when these heartaches come, I continue to drink to numb the pain.

I believe that's one of the reasons Dr. John decided to have me see my new therapist, Carla. She works with Post Traumatic Stress Disorder (PTSD) patients. The process seemed innocent enough. Carla would have me think about Bill, or an event, or nothing at all, while she tapped me in different parts of my back or the front of my legs. But her doing this caused a heightened reaction to these thoughts, and I would be severely affected throughout the rest of the day. Because of this difficulty, she was unable to work on this process with me because she said I was still too unstable to handle this therapy.

Friday, May 28, 2012—*The anniversary of our first meeting*

It hurts so much! As soon as I have a thought about our wonderful evening so long ago, when we first met, my memories flip to the horror of the accident and the loss of Bill. It's extremely difficult to handle this pain. It always makes me want to be where Bill is. But alone, on this very important anniversary, after a few drinks, I still try to let myself think about that night.

I had gone out with my brother, Roger, to a neighborhood bar. I knew a few of the guys—mostly because of Roger—so I was enjoying dancing with some of them. I had always been a good dancer, and I had learned that dancing was an easy way to get the attention of men.

As I turned while dancing, I noticed a man standing next to my brother. He was quite handsome, and much to my enjoyment, I saw that he was staring back at me. I finished the dance and walked over to say hi to my brother, as an excuse to meet this guy. He was tall—six feet two inches, which I loved since I'm tall at five feet seven inches. He had a solid build—not too skinny and not too heavy, with big broad shoulders—and nice features. I loved his beard.

The three of us talked for a while, but it didn't take long before Roger moved off elsewhere, so it was just Bill and me talking. It was amazing! We had no trouble coming up with different topics to talk about. We were finding out about each other, discussing what we liked, where we worked, things like that.

Roger came back to ask if Bill and I wanted to join his friends in a game of shots. I had never really understood the rules of these games, but I said I'd like to try it. Bill also quickly said yes to join us. I was a bit nervous because it didn't take much for me to get high, but I was having a good time.

What I didn't notice was how many times Bill lost. When he lost, he had to pay for the shots for everyone else. At a much later date, he told me he'd had to eat hotdogs and beans all week because he was broke from buying all those shots. I felt bad, but eventually that story became a good laugh with our friends.

When the game ended, Bill and I were talking again. This time we found out we both liked to camp, but we camped quite differently. When I camped with my friend Beth, I could only pack what would fit into my Camaro, so we would take along only what we needed to survive. We would take my tent, a large blanket (both for the bottom of the tent and for the beach later), sleeping bags, pillows (yes, we needed our pillows to survive), and flashlights. We filled Beth's cooler with simple cooking items such as hotdogs, hamburgers, eggs, and fresh vegetables. And we carried only the top screen from a grill, which we would put on the wood fire, along with one pan to cook in. And we each got a small bag to carry a few clothes plus our swimming suits and towels because we always camped near a lake so we could swim and sunbathe—Beth getting a wonderful bronze look, and me coming out red and splotchy.

Bill's camping was slightly different. He owned a pop- up camper. And, as I later learned, it carried everything— including the kitchen sink! He had a stove top, silverware, dishes, sheets, pillows, and who knew what else. He also liked to camp near a lake. But I didn't think he cared as much for the swimming and sunbathing as much as checking out the girls in their bikinis.

By the end of our camping discussion, I was teasing Bill that he was a sissy camper, and Bill was teasing me that if I ever went camping with a pop-up, I would never want to return to my tent. Later that summer, he turned out to be right. We went camping in his pop-up, and I had to stop saying he was a sissy camper, because now I was one also.

We eventually bought a new, slightly smaller camper that the two of us used often. Then we started bringing the kids, (my three step kids) then the kids brought their friends, then we brought our friends—Beth's family. Yes, it got pretty busy.

The funniest story we had camping was when we met a couple from Maryland. They had been traveling the states in one of those large campers. Alice told us that so many states were dry that they hadn't had a campfire at all on this trip. Well, Bill heard this and went back to our campsite. A while later he was walking down the path holding a piece of wood on fire with his safety gloves. Every campsite was watching and laughing, with Alice laughing the hardest. Bill set the fire in the pit and finished putting more wood in for a great fire. Alice said she would never forget watching Bill bringing her fire.

But back to the bar—it was closing time, and Bill was telling me that he had never planned on staying in the bar so long. He'd gotten off work at 10:30 p.m., and he was meeting someone who could get him inexpensive blank VHS tapes for his VCR. He told me he had groceries in his car for a late-night supper, and he hoped I would join him. He would do the cooking.

I hesitated at first because I had never left a bar with someone I had just met. But this situation felt different. I already felt quite comfortable with Bill, and Roger knew him.

I got in my car and followed Bill to his nearby apartment. It was a comfortable, casual upper flat—looking quite typical of a guy's decorating skills. I commented to Bill that he didn't have any pictures hanging on his walls and here I was an art major at college. Bill said that wasn't true, and quickly showed me his picture of beer bottles that he had torn from a magazine—torn, not cut—which he then taped to the wall.

Bill put on some music, and he started baking our steak and potatoes. I had never heard of baking a steak before, but Bill said he cooked his steak that way all the time. He seemed to know what he was doing, so I kept quiet. He even had stove-top stuffing. While all of this was cooking, he played some of his favorite songs he had taped on his cassette recorder, mainly late sixties and early seventies music, many of which were also my favorites. We were soon singing— sometimes goofy, sometimes serious—and then we started to slow dance to some of our favorites, including what was later to be our favorite band, *REO*.

Time to eat and it was delicious. I had never had a steak of this quality before. I was convinced he must be a good cook; I found out later, though, that he was only a good cook when he was baking a steak and potato. He could fry a hamburger and boil a hotdog, but it pretty much ended there.

After eating, I did the majority of the clean-up, but Bill joined in to wipe the dishes. I was immensely enjoying this evening. With the clean-up done, we went back to singing and dancing, although this time we added kissing and hugging. I felt wonderful in his arms, and his kisses were sweet.

We had no idea how fast time was moving until we noticed it was getting light outside. Oh my gosh! I still lived with my parents. I was too old for a curfew, but this could prove embarrassing. It was probably a good time to leave before my parents got up.

Bill walked me to my car and promised to call me later. That was great because I sure wanted him to call me. Luckily my parents were still asleep when I arrived home, so I quickly got into bed to dream about my wonderful evening with Bill.

Early June 2012

The anniversaries of Bill's accident and death were coming closer, and I continued to fall apart. I just didn't feel that I could handle them again. My drinking, my isolating, and my thoughts of hurting myself were all increasing. And my mental health team was noticing it. They strongly suggested that I should go into the psychiatric hospital. I started to realize that going into the hospital might be the best idea.

Thursday, June 14, 2012 — Inpatient psychiatric hospitalization

This was a huge decision for me. I had never been in a psychiatric hospital before, and the thought of it scared me. I was also worried about what family and friends might think about me. I knew that shouldn't be a worry, but I felt embarrassed. *Had I failed to be strong enough to go through this alone?* I wondered.

I decided I would only tell a few people that I had gone into the hospital. Of course I would need to tell Roger and his wife, Terry, because they would need to take care of my dog, Lady. Thank goodness Lady loved being at Roger's house, with his two dogs and cats to play with.

It was quite confusing to figure out what I should pack. It wasn't like going to a regular hospital—you could wear your own clothes. I packed a few things, and I asked Roger to drive me to my appointment with Dr. John. I would tell Dr. John I was ready to go into the hospital.

When I arrived in Dr. John's waiting room, my nervousness increased. I sat there wondering what would be happening to me soon. I walked into Dr. John's office, and immediately I started to cry. He must have seen the bag I was carrying, so he had a hint at what I was thinking. I just kept crying, saying I couldn't do this alone, that I was afraid I was going to hurt myself at home. He told me not to worry, that I would be safe in the hospital. He called the intake desk and told them I would be arriving in a few minutes. He explained to me that his administrative assistant would walk me over to the intake area and that I would see him tomorrow morning.

As we walked to the hospital, I felt very shaky. I just couldn't believe I was on my way to becoming an inpatient at a psychiatric hospital. It all seemed unbelievable. What was happening to my life? Where was Bill? Was this going to be it? I had a mouthful of questions, and I knew I didn't have the answers.

I felt very self-conscious when we entered the intake area. There were other people in the room—were they also entering the hospital? Were they visitors? More questions with no answers. No one seemed to want to look into the eyes of anyone else; most people were staring at the floor. Like me, maybe no one wanted to admit that they needed to go into the hospital.

I went to the registration window and tried to explain why I was there, that Dr. John was my doctor, and he had suggested I come here. She was all ready for me. She politely gave me multiple forms that I needed to complete.

Finally, the paperwork completed, I sat down and waited, getting more nervous as time went on. I started to wonder, *Just how big is this hospital? How busy are they? Will I have my own room?*

A door would occasionally open and someone would be called by their first name. The person would go through the door, and my wait would continue. I wondered what was wrong with the other people in the room. Were they crazy? Were they on drugs? Or were they going through a life trauma, like me?

I looked around and saw that most people had someone else with them, to help them. I felt so alone without Bill— he was always my protector, and I had felt safe with him. I prayed he was with me.

Finally they called my name, and I followed the nurse into another room. She asked me a series of additional questions. She also asked if I was suicidal, and I was embarrassed to say yes. She left for a while—I think to call Dr. John—and when she came back, I was escorted down the hall to my unit.

It was busy, with patients walking around, some staring at me. Again, I felt self-conscious, like the new kid on the block, scared and embarrassed. I told myself I wasn't crazy, but then what was I doing in a psychiatric hospital? Once again I wondered if these other patients were crazy. Would they try to hurt me? Yell at me? Would I be able to understand them? Too many unanswered questions.

Two friendly staff members from the nurses' station led me to my room. It was a clean, small room, and very bare. It had a bed, a lounge chair, a desk with a chair, and a small dresser with drawers. And, thank goodness, my own bathroom and shower. I had been hoping for that. What I wanted most was to be left alone, so I was glad to find out I wasn't going to have to share my room with another patient.

Standing there, I barely heard one of the staff members stating that I would be getting a body search. I was told to remove my outer clothes. After they searched the clothes, I was told to pull my bra up, and then pull my panties down. Like a robot, I did what they said. It all seemed like a bad dream, but it was over quickly, and I knew they were trying to make the process as comfortable as possible.

Next, they searched through my purse and gym bag, and I quickly saw that they were separating the "okay" pile with the "not okay" pile. Most of my belongings were in the "not okay" pile, such as my cell phone, prescriptions, sweat pants, pajama bottoms, and shoes. They told me I couldn't have any draw strings or shoe laces; they gave me hospital slippers for my feet. It was easy to figure out that all this was being done for my protection. They had to make sure I wouldn't injure myself. They even took my purse and gym bag. I was trying to figure out how I could hurt myself with them.

Next they gave me a folder that held paperwork that I was to look through. It explained some of the objectives of my visit. They told me that I was to participate in four group sessions a day, and Dr. John would visit me every morning. A medical doctor, a therapist, a case worker, and a dietitian would visit me the following day. They said that my nurse would bring in my medications, and then I should get some sleep. Then they left the room.

I sat on the bed and looked around. Life had changed so much. I wondered if I had made the correct decision to enter the hospital. After all, what did I really want but to be with

Bill? Well, I wasn't going to get to him from inside here. I felt so lonely. And now I was separated from Lady and from my home. I cried as I pictured Lady at Roger's house. She was probably having a fun time with Roger and Terry's dogs and cats. I was glad; I didn't want her to miss me. I was so relieved she was there, especially because I didn't know how long I was going to be in the hospital.

A nursing assistant came in to check my temperature and blood pressure. She finished quickly, and again I was alone in my room. No TV, no radio, no clock, no phone. I stared at the pictures on the walls; they were nice. But it made me nervous how quiet the room was. Would I be able to hear other patients in their rooms? I hoped not.

I quickly found out that I was being checked every fifteen minutes. A staff member would peek into my room through the gap in my door. I couldn't decide if that made me more nervous or if it made me feel safer. They put a sign on my door that said I was admitted today, and I was to rest. I didn't feel like resting, but I climbed into bed and closed my eyes.

Four days to the anniversary of Bill's accident. I felt too nervous to be tired, but I was going to give it a try.

A nurse entered my room with my nighttime medications. She said tomorrow I would get my medications from the nurses' station. She asked if I was hungry, and I told her no. I sure didn't feel like eating anything. And then I started crying. I think my emotions were finally ready to come out. The nurse tried to talk to me, but I kept crying. When I finally started to settle down, the nurse said we would talk more tomorrow, and she left.

I lay back in bed and closed my eyes again. I think I was more tired than I had realized, because I felt so drowsy. I think the medications were also taking effect. Good night to my first day.

I awoke startled, as a voice using a loudspeaker told us to come down to the nurses' station for breakfast. At least I was already dressed since I had lost my pajamas to the "not okay" pile. I quickly got up to go to the bathroom, splash some water on my face, brush my teeth, and comb my hair. Now I was nervously ready to get breakfast.

I went into the hallway and saw a clock: it was 7:30 a.m. No wonder I was tired. As I looked down the hallway, I could see a busy scene near the nurses' station, with everyone getting their breakfast trays from the staff. I slowly walked that way, feeling anxious.

Next to the nurses' station was a combination dining and TV area. I got my tray and went in. One table was open, and that was for me. Although I tried not to look at anyone else, my eyes started to wander the room. Some people were very quiet, looking like they wanted to be left alone. And then there were the others who were asking for things, talking loudly, jumping up and down to get one thing or another. My first guess was they must have been drug addicts because they seemed so hyperactive. They wanted to eat a lot and have a lot of coffee. Some of the patients were wearing their own clothes while others were wearing hospital gowns. I guess if someone had been unexpectedly admitted, they wouldn't have a change of clothes.

As I tried to eat my breakfast, some of the others were talking in street talk using a dialect that I was having trouble understanding. And there was more swearing than I was used to. A nurse told one of the patients to stop the foul language. I was glad for that.

As I finished eating, I saw some of the patients were having their temperature and blood pressure taken, so I hung around the nurses' station long enough to have a nursing assistant tell me she needed to get mine done also. I found out that having your vitals checked after eating was a regular morning routine. Then we were to go to the nurses' door for our medications. As I stood in line, I pictured myself as Jack Nicholson waiting for his pill from Nurse Ratchet in *One Flew over the Cuckoo's Nest*. Although, unlike Jack Nicholson, I wanted my medications—I was feeling very tense and knew they would help.

For day shift, I was assigned to a nurse named Linda, who seemed very nice. She gave me my medications and said she would be down to my room later so we could talk. We had to take our pills in front of the nurse, and again, I was thinking about the movie. I took my pills and decided to head back to my room to hopefully crawl back in bed and fall asleep.

I awoke to a knock on my door, surprised that I had already fallen asleep. I jumped up as Dr. John entered my room, and then I sat in the lounge chair as Dr. John pulled out the desk chair to sit on. He teased me about sleeping right after breakfast. I felt a little self-conscious, but he smiled and asked how I was doing so far. I told him how extremely nervous I was and started to cry. He told me he would be coming in every morning to check on me. He also explained that he would be giving all the orders for me, and my medications were to stay the same, at least for now.

We talked for a while, and then he got up to go. After he left, I reflected on our talk and felt thankful he was my doctor.

As I had been told, the morning was filled with visits from all the various staff members. The hospital's medical doctor gave me the once over. A unit therapist came in to get better acquainted with me, and a case worker came in to explain that she would be working with my insurance company and scheduling appointments with my psychiatrist and therapists once I was discharged. They were all nice, so that helped me feel a lot better.

When Linda came to see me, she sat down and explained that she wanted to get better acquainted with me. She had read my chart, so she knew my background. I cried while we talked; it was again hitting me in the face where I was. I told her I just wanted to die. She tried to console me and calm me down, and I explained what a shock it was for me to be in a psych hospital and how scared I was. She talked with me about a lot of things, and I slowly started to calm down.

Linda told me I would be starting my group sessions that afternoon. This also made me nervous—I really hadn't had a conversation with any of the other patients, and now I was going to be in a room with all of them.

When it was time for Linda to leave, she said we would talk again. I was glad about that. It felt good to have Linda to talk with.

After lunch, I went to the group therapy room. A couple of patients were already there, along with Julie, the therapist. I sat down and stared at the table top. A few more patients arrived, and Julie closed the door. I learned that the first step in group therapy was to fill out a form asking how you were doing on that day. I quickly saw I was being quite negative in most of my answers, but I was just trying to be honest. Then Julie started asking each patient about their answers. Yikes! I wasn't expecting to read what I'd written out loud. I got nervous all over again.

Surprisingly, it was interesting to listen to the other patients. Some were very quiet and gave short answers. Some were in the mood to talk and spent a large amount of time explaining their situations. Julie paid close attention to the group, especially asking questions of different people to try to get them to open up. Soon our time was up, and I was glad because I hadn't had to say too much.

The next session was going to be an outdoor break in a beautiful garden created by a staff worker. When I saw that it was surrounded by a high wall, I began to realize just how locked in we were. When I arrived the first night, the nurse used a combination to open the locked door. The door heading out to the garden was also locked. I realized I was in a jail of sorts. A nice jail, but a jail nonetheless.

The fresh air felt good as I went out into the garden. It was getting warmer outside, and a bit humid, but I still enjoyed being outside for a while. There was a walking track through the garden; I took two trips around it and then sat down in the gazebo, where Julie and a couple of the patients were sitting. We did some casual talking, and then it was time to go in for dinner.

I still kept to myself during the dinner meal. Some patients were watching TV, and some were just roaming around the room. After eating, I didn't know what I wanted to do. The TV programs that the patients were watching didn't interest me, and I didn't feel tired yet, so I didn't want to go back to my room. One of the staff—maybe noticing my confusion— told me there was a small library available if I would like a book. That sounded great to me. Surprise! The library was kept locked, but she let me in. I chose a book on religion, hoping to find some solace in it.

I headed back to my room with my book. I sat on the lounge chair, feet up on the bed, with the book in my lap. I read a couple of pages, and then I realized I was lost in my own thoughts. What a strange life I was leading now. Did Bill know I was going through all of this? I hoped he didn't. I wouldn't want him to feel bad. But my next thought was to wish Bill was always with me, knowing everything.

I realized I should call my best friend, Beth. She'd be mad at me if I didn't tell her where I was. We had looked after each other for many years, but I didn't think she was going to be ready to hear this story. There was a phone in the hallway for patient use, and luckily no one was using it, so I made my call. I must have sounded very upset when I told her where I was—she sounded concerned and said she would come visit me.

As I finished my conversation with Beth, I saw Roger coming through the unit door. I was glad to see him. We went back into my room to talk; I could see he was worried, but I couldn't do much about that. I knew if I put on my "smiley face," he would know it wasn't sincere. We talked for a while, and then he left, saying he'd be back tomorrow. *Always my big brother,* I thought.

I tried to go back to my book, but I was startled to hear a flute-like melody. *What was that?* I wondered. It sounded like it was coming from the next room. Maybe the patient next door had a tape player. But it sounded so real, like an American Indian song. I enjoyed it at first, but then it started to sound kind of eerie to me.

It was time for my pills, so I went to the nurses' station. Then I returned to my room. I went to bed hoping I'd fall asleep quickly like I had the first night, but the flute player was still playing. Unbelievable! I wasn't able to relax, and it didn't help that I had only my jeans to wear to bed. I was uncomfortable as I tossed and turned. But finally the sounds ended, and I relaxed and fell asleep.

Saturday, June 16, 2012

Another blast from the loudspeaker startled me awake again. Time for breakfast. I was learning this wasn't a place for lazy habits. They had a routine that they expected everyone to follow. This time, Dr. John arrived in the unit while I was still eating breakfast. At least he wouldn't catch me sleeping again.

We had another talk, and he took notes as usual. Dr. John was so easy to talk with; I could tell him most anything. He wanted to know how I was feeling. I told him I felt very sad and still wanted to die. He explained that dying would be difficult here—not impossible, but highly unlikely. He told me these rooms were built for safety's sake. I think I looked frustrated, because I saw a smirk on his face.

I wondered what happened during the weekends here. I quickly found out a weekend is pretty much the same as a weekday. We were still expected to go to our four group sessions per day. I really didn't like the sessions, but they were better than just sitting around, trying to read my book.

Julie was ready to hear my story today. She asked me to explain why I was here and what was happening in my life. I tried explaining about Bill, with tears welling up in my eyes. The group was very sympathetic to my circumstances, with a few of them trying to find ways to help me. They were the usual ideas: join groups, meet new people, and so on. Nothing new, but I appreciated that these people, with their own problems, were trying to help me. It was a reminder to me that I should be doing likewise.

Julie moved on to another person to ask questions, which pleased me. I was done talking.

It was interesting to watch how each day patients were being admitted and discharged. I was no longer the new kid on the block. A few new patients had been admitted during the night. One new patient was Rick, who joined the group today. Julie was looking for conversation, and today she picked Rick. He looked like a biker, and he seemed quite angry. He was talking about being a pilot and said that his plane had crashed and that he had died a couple of times on the night of the accident, trying to crawl toward help. I was hoping he would explain that in more detail, but he changed the topic to why he was here now. Something had made him angry enough to announce to his wife and sister that he was going to ride his Harley off a pier near his home. He didn't go through with it, but because his wife and sister got scared, they called 911. He was picked up for a possible suicide attempt and brought in. He was done talking for now, and the session soon ended.

I found his story interesting. Neither of us was here because of drugs or mental illness. Circumstances had led both of us on the path here. I wanted to hear more of his story.

When I headed down to my room to rest a bit before lunch, I watched a woman walking ahead of me. She went into the room next to mine, and I thought, *Hmm, now I know who was playing the music.* I decided that I wanted to figure out what was making that noise. But a rest and lunch came first.

At lunch, Rick sat down at the table with me. We started talking, and he wanted to know more about my story—which was a coincidence, since I wanted to hear more of his too. I told him about Bill's work injury and the day-to-day horror of hoping he would get well, only to watch him die after nineteen days.

Rick offered me sincere sympathy for my circumstances. And when I was done, he was in the mood to tell me his whole story. This was much better than going back to my room and reading my book.

He had been a commercial pilot, flying the large jets. But on the day of his accident, he was flying alone in a small plane. It was dark and rainy when his airplane's engine shut down. He attempted a landing and was skimming over the tops of some trees when his plane crashed, caught in the upper branches of a tree. He was severely injured, but his biggest problem was that he was high in the air, caught in that tree. He struggled to free himself, finally falling to the ground. He couldn't walk, so he dragged himself away from the tree as fast as possible, in case the plane also fell.

His body ached all over from his injuries, and he was bleeding. He was in a farm field at night, in the winter, with no help to be seen. He could make out a dim light across the field, so he decided that would be his best bet to aim for. He still couldn't walk, so he had to slowly crawl across the field, loosing blood and growing stiff from the cold. Along the way he passed out more than once, explaining that he must have been near death, because he remembered he had an out-of- body experience in which he looked down at his own body.

He finally reached the light, which was on the front of a barn. He didn't see any house close to it, so he decided to go into the barn to get some sleep until morning. It was hard to sleep because it was as cold in the barn as outside. At least the barn had hay to lie on and to cover him a little. In the morning he spotted the farmhouse and slowly made his way to it. He yelled for help, and the farm family heard him and helped him inside their home.

Eventually, after a hospital stay, he recovered from his injuries, but his trouble wasn't over. When the crash investigators checked out his airplane, they found broken glass from beer bottles. He explained to them that he hadn't had any to drink, that he had just bought it to have at home. Sadly, there was no way to prove that he hadn't drunk any. He lost his pilot's license—unfortunately, that meant he also lost his job.

His luck still didn't change. A couple of months later, he was near his motorcycle, again with a bag of full beer bottles. A police car pulled up to him, and the policeman had him do a sobriety test. He stated he hadn't planned on driving, but he still received a DUI.

After that, he was deep in depression and drinking often. Two days before he was admitted to the psych hospital, he had decided enough was enough. That's when he told his wife and sister that he was going to drive his bike off the pier.

He was very tense about all that had happened to him in the last few months. He told me he didn't know what type of work he would be able to do, because all of his experience had been in flying commercial jets. He bragged that he was quite a hot shot pilot. He had flown for so many years that many people in the field knew him. And now he was playing the role of stay-at-home dad. He said he loved his kids, but it was quite a difference for him. And his wife wasn't earning as much as he had, so it was a struggle financially too.

He then asked more about what had happened to Bill with his accident. He seemed quite interested and sympathetic, so I told him how Bill had been called into work during the night because of a rainstorm. He had just climbed down an underground ladder that led to the steam tunnels when a burst of steam filled the area. Bill managed to climb back up the ladder, but he was severely burned. He was rushed to a burn center in extremely critical condition. He was a strong, healthy guy, so he had managed to fight for survival for over two weeks. But his doctor discovered that Bill's small intestine had collapsed, and that was it. He died as I lay next to him in his hospital bed.

By the time I finished my story, the nursing assistant was calling everyone into the afternoon group session. When I walked into the room, the woman who occupied the room next to mine was already seated. I was going to be listening carefully to anything she had to say about music.

It took a while, but the conversation finally turned to my neighbor. She told a sad story of her older brother abusing her when she was quite young. She was older now, probably around sixty, and she was still too intimidated to tell anyone, including her own parents. As she grew older, she believed that her parents had to know something about it, but she still didn't tell them for fear that they would side with her brother. She had carried the trauma with her all these years. She was trying to get up the courage to have a family meeting here at the hospital. We were all encouraging her to do it, but she was done talking. The session ended with no mention of music.

A little break, and we had to return for the next session. The last session of the day was craft time. At first it sounded so silly, and I thought, *How will coloring pictures help when we have all these problems?* But I quickly saw that as we chose what project to work on, the conversation flowed around the table. *That was pretty smart*, I thought. And, as I had hoped would happen, Julie asked the woman next door to me if she would play her recorder for us tomorrow. At first I thought she meant the type of recorder that plays cassettes (yes, that idea shows my age), but as they talked I remembered there was an instrument called a recorder—similar to a flute. That was it!

It was mentioned that she had to get special approval from her doctor to bring it in. I thought to myself that she should have gotten permission from her neighbors as well. Was I going to hear that music every night?

The crafts session ended, and I realized there were a lot more patients in the unit than had attended the groups. I asked one of the staff about that. He said even though they wanted everyone to attend, not everyone went to group. Some patients just returned to their rooms. I quickly learned to follow the schedule, because people seemed to be discharged sooner if they did what they were supposed to do. And I didn't want to miss out on anything that might help me.

Beth came to visit me; I showed her to my room and told her some of my adventures. It was easier to laugh about it when I had company. But the minute she left, my mood dropped immensely. Tomorrow is the anniversary of the last day I spent with Bill before he was called into work that horrible night. I knew I'd be thinking about that.

Roger also came to visit again tonight. This time we stayed out in the group area, and I introduced Roger to my new friend Rick. I knew Rick wouldn't mind telling his story again, and I knew it would be more interesting for Roger than sitting in my room. I was right—the two of them had a good talk. But time passed quickly, and Roger left for the night. I needed to get my pills and hopefully get an early night's sleep, so I wouldn't be thinking about our last night.

The woman next door was playing her recorder again, but somehow, knowing where it was coming from helped. I was able to ignore it and fall asleep.

Dr. John told me he would be discharging me today. He felt I had calmed down and would probably prefer to be back home with Lady.

I didn't think about the date while Dr. John was with me, but later I realized if I was discharged today, I would be facing the three-year anniversary of Bill's accident by myself. I cried and cried, knowing I didn't feel strong enough to handle it alone. I talked with my evening nurse, Jane, who was just coming onto her shift. She saw how upset I was and said she was going to talk about this with my daytime nurse, Linda.

About half an hour later, Jane came into my room and told me I would be staying another couple of days. They had talked with Dr. John, and they all agreed I shouldn't be going home right on the anniversary. He hadn't realized we were right on top of those dates.

I felt relieved, but I was still in tears; my emotions rushed to the surface. I worried about going home when I knew I wasn't any better and was still having thoughts of hurting myself. Jane came to check on me and saw me sobbing. She stayed for a while to help comfort me. I knew I couldn't stay in the hospital forever, but I was still so uncertain what I might do. I missed being able to have a drink like I could at home. Those drinks seemed to numb me enough to get me through the rough spots. I knew Dr. John's opinion on that subject—he had explained to me many times that the alcohol kept my medications from fully doing their job. But he did understand why I did it.

In the evening session, Rick announced in group that he no longer wanted to kill himself. He said he never really felt he wanted to go through with it. He was just angry at what was happening to him. He also explained this to his doctor, and he was being discharged right after group. But before he left, he gave me a big hug and told me to hang in there. It was strange to find a common spirit to talk with at the hospital. I was going to miss our conversations; they had made the time go by faster.

As the evening went on, I knew I was glad to be staying here a little longer. In the evening, Jane came back to visit me again. She sat a while with me as a sobbed intensely, thinking about Bill's accident. I was finally worn out enough to fall asleep.

Tuesday, June 19, 2012

As usual, Dr. John came by in the morning to see how I was doing. He apologized that he hadn't noticed that yesterday was the start of the anniversary dates, or he wouldn't have suggested sending me home. He said he would see how I was doing tomorrow. I thanked him, and after our session I went back to the groups. It was hard concentrating on what other people were saying when I was thinking about Bill's accident, but I was glad to be here for another day.

Wednesday, June 20, 2012

Dr. John came in early and asked how I was doing this morning. I told him I was calmer than last night, and my thoughts of suicide had decreased. After talking with me for a while, Dr. John said I could be discharged today. I was to return to my outpatient visits with him and my therapist, Gregg. I felt relieved that I was going home—especially to see Lady. But I knew I was still very fragile. This time of year was horrible for me. I would be thinking about Bill's accident until after July 6, the date of his passing.

I gathered my things quickly and headed for the nurses' station. I found out I didn't need to hurry. They still had to complete all my paperwork, so I would be attending the morning sessions.

I called Roger and let him know I'd be released today. He told me to call him when I was ready, and he'd come to take me home, with Lady in the back seat. That was the best part. Being with Lady tonight.

Thursday, June 21, 2012

It was strange being home. One day you're being watched every fifteen minutes; the next day you're alone at home, free to do whatever you want. And I chose to think about Bill— while petting Lady. It was good to have Lady with me, but I still felt very alone.

Friday, June 22, 2012

I loved being back in my house, but I knew I wasn't out of the woods yet. It was two weeks until the date of Bill's passing. I still felt very tense and I still didn't want to be here. I wanted to be with Bill. I knew that kind of thinking was what had put me in the hospital in the first place. This could be a vicious cycle.

Sunday, July 1, 2012

Five years since mom died. It feels so long ago, but I greatly miss her. She and I had such a wonderful relationship since my childhood. Just that right balance between parent and friend. We loved to do things together. But if I was busy with my friends, she was fine with that also. We didn't see a lot of each other while Bill and I were dating. But she was okay with that too. She always wanted the best for me.

Three years after Bill and I were married, Bill decided my parents needed to move in with us. My dad had experienced a severe stroke. After a long stay in the hospital, he was in a wheelchair. It was growing more difficult for my parents to manage this situation. Bill and I bought a small ranch-style home and moved my parents into the main floor, while Bill and I lived in the fixed-up basement. I will always remember, just days after we moved in, my mom and I were both downstairs doing our laundry. The two of us were talking as we worked, when all of a sudden she got this smile on her face and told me how happy she was to be doing our wash together. It was such a nice moment to hear her say that. And I will always remember that smile.

Tuesday, July 3, 2012

I keep remembering being with Bill in his hospital room on his last July 3rd. While I stood next to his bed, with my hand on his head, I was able to look out the window and see the lake. It reminded me of all the times we rode the motorcycle down to the lakefront to see the Fourth of July fireworks. Now I wish I could close off my ears so I wouldn't have to hear the fireworks from my house ever again. Going to bed earlier wouldn't help either. They would probably still wake Lady or me.

Wednesday, July 4, 2012

Bill and I experienced so many wonderful Fourth of July holidays, whether just the two of us or with large groups of people. And now I couldn't stand to think of what day it was. There was no Fourth of July for me anymore. Between Mom's and Bill's deaths being so close to the date, it felt disrespectful to celebrate. I tried to tell as many people as possible to not invite me to anything or come over. It was a very sad day for me.

Friday, July 6, 2012

Three years since Bill's passing. I can't believe that much time has gone by. I didn't want to live past the first year, then the second, and now the third. It doesn't seem to matter how much I pray to God to take me... He just isn't doing it.

I had my appointment with my therapist, Gregg, today. I cried through the whole hour, and Gregg showed great concern. I had just been released from the hospital, and I wasn't doing any better. He wondered if I should go back in, but I said no. I wanted to go to the cemetery and then go home. I wanted to be with Lady. I wanted to be in the house where I had lived with Bill.

Gregg reminded me of our agreement: If I was going to do myself harm, I would either go to the hospital or call someone. I agreed again.

Back home, I decided to drink to numb some of this pain. I had been told numerous times by Dr. John and Gregg that the alcohol would only numb me for a while, and then I would feel worse. And the alcohol didn't let the medications do their full job. But when I feel so much pain I can't stand it. I was drunk by the time I went to our bedroom. It was hard to face the empty bed, and it took a lot of sobbing before I fell asleep.

Saturday, July 7, 2012

I have to get through this weekend. It's going to be difficult. I still choose to be alone—but of course with Lady. I always seem to feel closer to Bill when I'm suffering. I've discussed this often with Dr. John and Gregg, and they try to explain that I don't have to suffer to be close to Bill. I've heard that many times, but it doesn't seem to matter. I still do it.

Sunday, July 8, 2012

People at church could see I was having a hard time. Some people were there when Bill was still with us, but now there are a handful of people who joined the congregation after Bill was gone. Some of them heard the story from someone else, but at times I would need to explain why I was crying. Today there was no hiding it. I kept crying.

I came home, alone as usual, and started drinking again. Once again I can't face the pain.

Wednesday, July 11, 2012

At my appointment with Dr. John today, my drinking became a matter for discussion. He decided I should join a group that meets at the hospital three mornings a week, for two weeks. It's called the Intensive Outpatient Program (IOP). There's one for substance (drinking and drug) abuse, and there's one for mental health. I told him, if I have to do this, I'd prefer the mental health group. But he told me, no, he wants me to go to the substance abuse one. It isn't often that Dr. John orders me to do something; this was one of those times. He wasn't giving me a choice. He would set it up and I would be starting next week. Yuck!

Friday, July 13, 2012

I told Gregg that I had to start this program, and he agreed with Dr. John that it would be a good idea. I guess there's no way out of this.

Monday, July 16, 2012

When I walked into the building where the IOP group sessions are held, I was surprised to see that so many of the patients attending this group are in their twenties. That's sad.

I sat through the first lecture and was immediately bored. I have no desire to find out more about substance abuse. And a lot of the patients attending had abused drugs, so I didn't relate to that at all. But I sat and listened. We had a break after the first lecture, and I couldn't figure out where all of the patients had gone until I looked out a window. There was a picnic table close to the building, and they were all outside, smoking cigarettes. Now I really didn't relate to this group. They had shifted from one addiction to another.

In the next part of the session, we broke into smaller groups, each with its own therapist. Every group session began with the patients stating how long they had been off alcohol or drugs. Almost everyone in the group knew the exact date they stopped. We would go around the room, listening as people stated, "I've been clean for two weeks," or twenty-six days, or forty-four days. I had no idea how long it had been since I last had a drink. So I would just say something like one month.

Next we had to discuss how we were doing and explain our addiction. I wasn't sure what I wanted to say. I was guessing that most of the patients craved their alcohol or drug. I didn't. I was using alcohol to self-medicate, to ease the pain.

I felt nervous explaining my circumstances to this group. I briefly went through my story as I watched the faces on the patients. They knew I was different. Some even tried to suggest solutions for some of my problems. That was sweet, but nobody came up with anything different from what I had already tried to do. I wasn't ready for two weeks of this.

Wednesday, July 18, 2012

At my appointment with Dr. John, I let him know that I didn't relate to the IOP group, and I explained my reasons. He smiled and said it would be over in a couple of weeks. So much for trying to get out of it again.

Thursday, August 2, 2012

Yay! Today was the last day of the IOP group—it's been two weeks. Maybe I got something out of it, but it was just too different from my situation. I sat in the discussion group feeling so good it was my last session. And then it hit. The therapist started asking me questions, probably because I was being so quiet. She started with the question of never drinking again. I knew that wasn't me. Yes, I agreed I needed to have less, but I wasn't ready to not have anything to drink, ever. Yes, my doctor had explained that drinking and medications didn't mix well, so I was going to try to have less than I had been having before.

The therapist asked if I had any alcohol in my house. I said yes. She told me to throw it down the sink. I said no, that when I have company, if they want a drink I want to be able to serve them. Then the therapist let me have it. She explained if I wasn't ready to throw it all away, I wasn't ready to change my ways. I explained, as I had many times in the group meeting, that I don't crave alcohol; I don't use it all the time. And when I do, it's only to relieve my pain.

That didn't go over well with the therapist. I hoped she would go onto another patient, and thank goodness, she finally did.

When the session was over, the therapist checked to see if it was anybody's last session. She didn't mention me, so I told her it was my last session. She told me, no, I needed more time in the class. I explained that my doctor told me I would need to attend for two weeks. And I had completed that. We went back and forth, and finally, I just said I was done today. She told me if I left I wouldn't have passed the group. I said that was fine; I was done.

I left feeling so tense—I just didn't feel this group was able to understand my circumstances. But I was done, thank goodness.

Wednesday, August 8, 2012

At my appointment with Dr. John, I explained how I had ended my IOP session. I could tell he wasn't thrilled. Of course he had hoped this would help me more. But what was done, was done. We went on to discuss other things.

Mid-August 2012

As the month has progressed, I've been feeling worse again. Home life isn't going well. I've been having trouble getting anything accomplished, inside or outside. My yard needs a lot of work, but I just don't feel like doing it. A couple of times I went outside to pull some weeds, but I would begin to feel anxious and I would quit. I remembered Bill working alongside me on one of his own projects. Or sitting on the swing with a Pepsi, waiting for me to stop and join him. We would sit on the swing together, with my head usually pressing into his shoulder. We would talk about all kinds of things or we would just gaze into our backyard, or upward, looking at our large maple trees. Either way, it was delightful being together. And now all of that is gone.

Late August 2012

I've been growing more and more tense. It builds in my stomach and chest, to a point that all I can think about is wanting to die. Dr. John and Gregg have noticed how my depression has been worsening, and they've let me know their worries.

They are suggesting that I go into the hospital again. I just don't want to go. I'm not ready. And I'm embarrassed. I managed to hide my last hospital visit from most of my friends and family. But I don't know if I'd be able to do that again.

Unfortunately, I know they're right. I'm feeling more depressed and it's getting harder to function because of it. My thoughts of Bill are continuous. And they aren't happy memories; they're sad memories. They've been dragging me down.

Sunday, September 9, 2012 — Second hospital stay

I finally gave in. I knew my emotions were getting too much for me to handle. I was thinking about being with Bill every day. So I asked Roger if he would drive me to the hospital entrance. I again wanted to walk in alone. And I think I was trying to hide how upset I was from Roger.

Here I was again, walking down the hallway toward the intake area. Everything has changed so much since I lost Bill. I was living in such a loving environment, with hardly a worry in sight. Then it all changed. I felt so alone. So sad. I wanted it to end.

I entered the intake waiting room and went to the reception window. Same routine as last time. I had to complete the stack of paperwork, go through the interview questions, and admit that I wanted to kill myself. I couldn't believe I was here for a second time.

I was assigned to the same unit as last time. I was glad, since I wanted as little change as possible. A couple of the staff recognized me, and sadly welcomed me back. I had to go through the same admitting procedure as before. I again went through the motions, trying not to think too much. This time I had tried to pack things they wouldn't take away. When it was done, they again told me the nurse would be in to give me my medications. And after that I should try to get some sleep. Tomorrow would be busy. But at least I would be seeing Dr. John.

Monday, September 10, 2012

I awoke early to the announcement of breakfast. I finished getting dressed just in time for a nurse to say Dr. John was here.

That was good news. He walked in my room, looking quite sullen. That was unlike his usual smile to greet me.

He explained that he wouldn't be able to be my admitting doctor this time. His own doctor had found a cancer in him, so he would need to go through all the necessary treatments.

I stared at him in shock. I couldn't talk, but I could feel tears welling up in my eyes.

He said the doctor who would be covering his patients was Dr. Steven. He explained that he and Dr. Steven had the same philosophy, and that I would be fine in his care. He tried to put on a good face, saying he had every intention of being back in a couple of months.

A couple of months? I repeated in my head. *That can't be. I can't do this without Dr. John.* But I didn't want him to see just how upset I was. After all, he was the one who had to face this enormous challenge.

Getting up, he apologized to me, saying he never thought this would happen. I thought I saw a tear in his eye. I wanted to reply to that, but he was already leaving the room. As the door closed behind him, I burst out crying and lay back on my bed, not knowing what to do. I didn't want to be here without Dr. John. But I knew it would be difficult to leave. I was more upset than before, and probably more likely to harm myself if I tried to go home. I needed to stay.

Most of the morning went by with me still crying. The therapist and the nurses tried talking with me; some of them were also worried about Dr. John. All I knew was that Dr. John wasn't here, and I was already scared of Dr. Steven— even before I met him.

Come afternoon, I had lunch. Like last time, I was surrounded by people I didn't know, nor cared to know. I just wanted to be by myself. I didn't want to talk with anyone. I was about to return to my room when a doctor called out my name.

There he was—Dr. Steven. He stood straight-backed, wearing a suit and shirt pressed so carefully I wouldn't be able to find a wrinkle if I tried. He pointed to one of the rooms that I hadn't been in last time. He opened a door, and I entered the room with him behind me.

We sat in the two chairs set up for conversation. I felt scared and sat very quietly, waiting for him to talk. But again, tears were forming in my eyes.

He introduced himself, saying Dr. John had talked with him, and he of course had read over my chart. He started by telling me I was taking a lot of medications. I thought that sounded weird, as if I had decided on my own to take these drugs. He said he was going to be making some changes, and I grew even more worried. Great! Now I was going to have to face medication changes—and it clearly sounded like he was going to decrease my medications. So much for his having the same philosophy as Dr. John. We talked a little more, and he said that was all for today. I headed back to my room to cry again.

Later in the day, the nursing assistant came to my room to tell me Roger was here to visit. I was glad to see him, but I felt embarrassed having him visit me at the hospital. I felt so weak. But I talked about my day, and how upset I was that Dr. John wasn't here and that I would be having another psychiatrist.

I could see on his face that he was worried about how I was doing. But luckily he decided to cheer me up and started telling his usual funny stories, so we had a good visit. He left when it was time for my evening pills.

That evening, when I got my meds at the nurses' station, I saw that Dr. Steven had cut back on the dosage of a pill that helped me sleep. It had taken Dr. John a long time to find the dosage to make me sleep. Now I was here in the hospital, and it had already been changed. I went back to my room worrying about whether I was going to be able to fall asleep. No surprise—I tossed and turned for hours.

I was angry; I didn't need things to get even worse than before. Again I was crying, wishing I was home and worrying about Dr. John. *What if he never comes back to work?* I thought, agonizing about everything. The nursing assistants that check each patient every fifteen minutes were watching me and occasionally asking if I needed anything. I wanted to say, *Yes, I need more drugs!* But I controlled myself. I didn't want to create trouble for myself while I was in the hospital.

The more I thought about it, the more I realized that, even when I got out of here, I would be Dr. Steven's patient until Dr. John returned. I had been seeing Dr. John since Bill had passed. This was horrible. At least I would still be seeing Gregg, my therapist. There was comfort in that.

And somehow, finally, I fell asleep.

Tuesday, September 11, 2012

I awoke to the breakfast call, feeling very tired and knowing today would be a busy day. I would see my therapist, the medical doctor, the nutritionist, and the case worker, and I would start going to my four daily group sessions.

I didn't want to face anything. I wished I could just stay in my room, but that wouldn't help. Being in the hospital means following a very strict schedule. The last thing they want you to do is stay in your room all day, and I understand that.

The therapist was the same one I had when I was hospitalized in June. That's good; I liked her. I told her what happened with Dr. John, but she already knew. I started crying again, and she was so sympathetic that I settled down some. She didn't know Dr. Steven very well, but had heard he was very good. I didn't know if I believed her or not, but I didn't ask her anything else.

Dr. Steven saw me near the nurses' station, so we went to the same room for our talk. I told him I had trouble sleeping last night, but he still sounded quite adamant about lowering the volume of drugs I was taking. I mostly listened, knowing I wasn't going to make an impact on him. The session was soon over.

I went to my first group session. Again, I had the same therapist as last time—Julie. I was glad for that also. I came into the room and said hello, feeling a bit foolish to be back again so soon. I wondered how often people returned to this hospital. *Probably often*, I thought. Julie gave me a break and just let me say my name to the group today. Thank goodness. I wasn't up to explaining my whole story.

A few of the other patients were talking quite a bit in the group. One, named Mary, was quite funny. She had a quick smile and laugh. She was pretty, with beautiful thick red hair, but she didn't seem concerned that it hadn't been combed in what looked like quite some time. I watched her, thinking her laughter was covering something she wasn't ready to talk about. I decided she would be interesting to talk with.

After group, it was time for lunch. I noticed on the TV in the common area that they were showing remembrances of 9/11. Eleven years had passed since terrorists had flown commercial airplanes into the World Trade Center and the Pentagon. I remembered that I felt so sorry for those people… for the office workers, the firemen, the policemen, and their families. At the time, I couldn't imagine how those family members must have felt. Now I felt like a kindred spirit. I had also lost my husband to a disaster without any warning. I wondered how those families were coping, and then I went back to my room and cried before the next group meeting.

This time in group I was asked to talk about my situation. I gave a brief explanation of what happened to Bill, how I couldn't accept what happened, and that I was on my own now. I felt exhausted and was ready to be alone in my room again. Luckily, Julie was ready to go to the next person. And soon the session was over.

This time, as I sat alone while eating dinner, Mary joined me. She was quite talkative, so it was easy listening to her. She had a colorful story to tell as she shared with me her desire for sex. She had a big smile on her face and enjoyed telling me about some of her escapades. It made me wonder why she was in the hospital. But when her guard was down, she shared more of her story. Her husband had divorced her. They shared a daughter, and because of her behavior, her husband had full custody. She was still in love with her ex-husband and was devastated that she couldn't be with her daughter. She had thoughts of suicide. I couldn't believe this friendly, smiling woman had so much sadness in her.

I went to the nurses' station for my medications. I noticed I didn't have as many pills as the night before. Dr. Steven had decreased more of my medications again. I felt angry and worried. *Now I'll have even more trouble falling asleep*, I decided.

I lay in bed, tossing and turning again, feeling more like crying than sleeping. It took quite a while, but I finally fell asleep.

Wednesday, September 12, 2012

Again, that loud call for breakfast. I was never going to get used to waking up like that. But there was no choice; I had to get up and get dressed. This morning I decided to use the shower. I was so cold. The water pressure wasn't very strong, so the bathroom didn't fill up with warm steam. I hurried as fast as I could so I could get dressed and be warm again.

This time I joined Mary at her table. She was being funny as usual. After she finished her breakfast, she was still hungry, so she was asking everyone if they were going to eat all their food. Yuck—but she was funny. She was pretty sure that one of her medications was causing her to be extremely hungry. She said she had already gained weight.

It was time for the first group therapy session. This time, a woman named Kathy entered the room in a wheelchair. She had lost one of her legs as a child. But she, like Mary, had a big smile and was very friendly to everyone. And just like Mary, I wondered why she was here. She seemed to be in such good spirits.

Even as she talked in group, it was hard to understand what was wrong. She was married with three children. She talked about them with enthusiasm and didn't seem to have anything to complain about. *She must be hiding something*, I guessed.

As I was walking back to my room after group, I saw Dr. Steven, who was here to see me. Again I felt nervous, and again, I was fighting tears. He wanted to know how I was doing with the medication changes. I told him again that I was having trouble sleeping, but it didn't seem like he was going to do anything about it. He reminded me to go to all the group therapy sessions, and I told him I would. With that, our session was over.

Mary and I were becoming friends, and as we sat at a table for lunch, we invited Kathy to join us. The two of them were definitely cheering me up with all of their stories. It was easier to deal with being in the hospital with some people to talk with.

Roger visited me later and brought me a soda and candy bar. I was missing both of these, so they were very welcome. I told him about my new friends and how they were making it easier to be here. Of course, Roger was more interested in hearing whether the treatment was helping me. I told him that it was very difficult with a different psychiatrist, especially when he kept lowering my meds, and I was having so much trouble sleeping.

Roger seemed pleased about the meds being lowered, saying that might be a good thing for me. But he was sorry I couldn't sleep. I told him one good thing was that I was listening to other people and their problems, instead of always thinking of myself.

Time again for meds, bed, and again—a continuous struggle to get to sleep.

Thursday, September 13, 2012

The days are becoming a blur. Session after session.

At lunchtime today, Mary, Kathy, and I were having a silly time together. I looked up and saw Dr. Steven. Time for my session with him.

We started our talk, and he commented that I looked better today, the way I was talking with other patients and smiling. He went on to explain how important it was for me to socialize. I knew that, but it was all momentary. As soon as I stopped talking with someone, I'd be depressed again. So I let him know that I was enjoying them, but it wasn't changing how I felt about losing Bill and being lonely and depressed. Again, I told him I was having trouble sleeping, but he didn't say much about that.

The rest of the day seemed to go on and on.

Friday, September 14, 2012

I noticed I was starting to get dizzy. I tripped over things a couple of times. It reminded me of my accident a year and a half ago, when I fell and ended up in the hospital with a cracked skull and two subdural hematomas. I couldn't walk very well after that, and I was always feeling dizzy, like I was going to bump into things or fall down. Now it was happening again. It worried me. *Is it me or the medication changes?* I wondered.

But at least my two friends were continuing to keep me company, and having them in the group sessions was great. They talked a lot, which helped me—probably because I didn't have to talk as much.

Kathy had told her story. She was from Wisconsin, but she had married a man who worked for the Air Force. The base was in Texas, so she, her husband, and their two children had moved near the base. She had been very sad about moving because she had to leave family and friends behind. No one lived very close to her now, and she wasn't making any friends. She was mostly at home with her children. She said by the time her husband got home each night, he just ate and went to bed. And it didn't help that she was in a wheelchair. It limited where she could go. She thought about suicide— another girl with a big smile that wasn't happy. We seemed to be a threesome, hiding our pain.

Roger was still visiting me every night. It was a nice change of the daily pace, actually talking to someone familiar. And he would tell me stories about what was happening with Lady and his pets. Lady was always curious about the cats. And one of them, named Bee Gee, seemed curious about her. They would play with each other, licking each other's faces and touching each other. I hoped I could see them do it sometime.

Roger left, and I went to bed, facing another restless night.

Saturday, September 15, 2012

I've been here a week already. In my session with Dr. Steven this morning, he didn't mention anything about my going home, and I didn't want to ask.

I seem to be having trouble with my concentration, but I'm still going to sessions. Since the weather is so nice, they let us enjoy the fenced-in garden area. It's nice to get outside for a while every day, but I gave up walking around the path. I felt too tired and too uncertain on my feet.

Being locked in is difficult to take some of the time. I try not to think about it; I don't need any more tension. And I always have Mary and Kathy here to lift my spirits.

Sunday, September 16, 2012

I don't remember most of the day, but I do remember our time at supper. The girls and I were getting silly as usual. We were laughing as Mary checked everywhere for extra food again. Her hunger seems to be getting worse. She was even ordering extra food on her menu. And she's been gaining weight. I feel sorry for her trying to wear the clothes she brought. They're so tight now.

After dinner we were all watching TV. I was trying to get through some of the chairs, and I tripped and fell over. I didn't hurt myself, and the girls had fun laughing at me. *Why am I so clumsy?* I pondered. What I didn't know then was that Roger, Beth, and a couple of friends from church had come to visit and saw me so dizzy, tripping over things. When I was told this later, I vaguely did remember them being there, but that was it. Roger told me later that he was so worried that he almost threw me over his shoulder and carried me out. Thank goodness he didn't.

When I went to my room, I saw a sign on my door saying to be careful, patient falls. It seemed weird that I had a notice on my door like that, but I just ignored it and went into my room. I don't really remember going to bed. But I remember waking up and needing to go to the bathroom. When finished, I left the bathroom and headed back to my bed. Then I saw one of the nursing assistants sleeping on a chair in the corner. I remember thinking that was odd, but I just went back to sleep.

Monday, September 17, 2012

More group sessions, more outside visits to the garden, more visits with Dr. Steven. It's all a blur. I do remember another woman, Cindy, joining our threesome. She has a noticeable mental problem—slow with speech, and doesn't say very much. But she's so sweet. She has a serious face, but when someone says something that's even a little funny, she starts laughing. The first time she burst out laughing, it was very unexpected and caused the rest of us to start laughing also.

Tuesday, September 18, 2012

Nothing but vague memories of us girls laughing and talking together, and vague memories of us talking in the group sessions. I mostly just listened to the others. They were so funny. I don't remember meeting with Dr. Steven. I'm sure I did, but I have no memory of it.

Wednesday, September 19, 2012

We girls were chatting as usual at a table in the TV room. Up until now, Cindy has been very quiet. But today she must have felt comfortable with us, because she started to explain her story. She is married, which surprised me. She relies on her husband for day-to-day living arrangements, and they've been very happy, but now he's telling her that maybe she should live in a mental care facility. She is so saddened by this—she thought things were okay between the two of them. Tears were in her eyes as she told her story. It was so sad.

Thursday, September 20, 2012

I feel a little clearer today. I took a shower and joined the group. A lot of new faces today. And I don't see some of the patients who've been here. Some patients only stay a couple of days. Since I've been here so long, I notice everyone's comings and goings.

In the group session, I seemed to be paying better attention today. I was trying to participate more, and I listened carefully while Mary talked. She sounded like she was falling apart. She kept repeating to herself that she missed her daughter. She had a lawyer trying to help her, but nothing seemed to be improving as far as her visitations.

A couple of new ladies have been admitted to the hospital, so we have quite a group now. I think the whole unit is full.

Friday, September 21, 2012

Again, I feel like I have better concentration. During my session with Dr. Steven, he told me I've been delusional the last few days—but that I'm improving. I don't remember being that way, but that could explain my forgetfulness. I feel angry, because I'm guessing the medication changes caused this.

Saturday, September 22, 2012

Dr. Steven came to visit today, and we discussed different treatment options for helping me to get better. He asked if I knew about ECT treatments. I asked if those were shock treatments, and he said yes, but they were very different from what they used to be. It scared me, and I didn't want anything to do with that. He told me he was going to get me a movie about ECT, to show me it wasn't like it used to be. I left the session feeling very nervous. I was sure I wouldn't have any of those treatments.

A nurse gave me the movie on ECT, and the girls and I watched it. Wow! It was a 1960s-looking movie showing the doctors applying the apparatus to the patients. No way!

Sunday, September 23, 2012

Sundays are almost always very quiet. I'm hoping to go home soon. I miss my dog, Lady, so much.

During lunch, I asked the girls if any of them had experienced ECT. Mary and Cindy both had these treatments. Mary said it helped for a while, but then the beneficial effects went away. Cindy said she didn't feel any different after the sessions. That was what I wanted to hear. Verification that I would never allow it.

Mary has been talking to her doctor for a few days about going home. She needs to talk with her lawyer about her daughter, and she wants to get visitation rights to see her daughter. She misses her so much. It sounds like she'll be leaving soon.

Monday, September 24, 2012

Mary went home this morning. I will miss her. It doesn't seem the same around here without her.

During my session with Dr. Steven, I told him I don't want the ECT treatments. He asked me to keep it in mind. I pretended to act like I would think about it, but I'm sure I won't try it.

Just after dinner this evening, all the lights went out, and it was pitch black in the building. The staff told us all to stay in the dining area. They checked all the rooms to make sure no one was alone in the dark. Everyone got quite excited, and some got loud. Others, like me, sat quietly. I felt nervous because they were unable to disperse medications without electricity. That would be an ugly situation—all of us without our medications. I was thinking about the movie *One Flew over the Cuckoo's Nest* again.

After two hours, the lights finally came on, and we were able to get our medications. I noticed this time I was receiving more of my original nighttime medications. That didn't make sense to me. First he took me off some of the medications, and then he added them back. If only Dr. John were here.

Tuesday, September 25, 2012

In my session with Dr. Steven, he told me I'm being discharged from the hospital today. Tomorrow I'm supposed to join the Partial Hospitalization Program. He said they meet from 9:00 a.m. to 3:00 p.m., Monday through Saturday. They have lectures in the morning and group sessions in the afternoon.

I don't like the idea, but he wasn't asking me if I want to join the partial program; he was telling me I have to. I know it's best to just go along with it. At least he isn't talking about ECT anymore. He also mentioned that maybe I should stay on campus and live in one of the housing units. I told him no, I want to go home and live with my dog. Thank goodness he didn't push it.

I let Roger know that I'm being discharged and that I need him to come pick me up. I'm glad to be going home; it's been a long fifteen days. But I'm scared now to think what partial is going to be like.

Wednesday, September 26, 2012

My first day in partial. I arrived to a lecture-style set-up in a room on the other end of the hospital building, packed full of patients. I didn't expect so many people; it had me feeling nervous. I kept quiet, trying to get used to the group. Two therapists were in front of the room, taking turns calling out patients' names. When called, they asked how the person was doing. "How were you last night? Did you have breakfast?" Those types of questions. Some were answered quickly, but if the patient seemed to be in difficulty, the therapist would ask more questions.

Then one of the therapists would start the lecture section. They would have one topic such as depression or anger. And they would talk for about an hour on that subject. Then another therapist would come in and lecture on their topic. Some of this was interesting, but most of it to me was very basic. I was bored and I was upset. I didn't want to be there.

During the lecture time, doctors would arrive at the door, signaling a patient to come out of the room. They would have a short session with each patient. When Dr. Steven arrived, I left the group to join him in a different room. He asked questions about how I was doing. I still felt nervous due to moving from inpatient care at the hospital to outpatient care in this program. I'm used to Dr. Steven's style now, though. He really is a nice man. I just don't always agree with him. But today it felt good talking with him. I could tell he didn't think I was doing very well, because he talked with me for quite a while before sending me back to the lecture room.

Instead of listening to the lecture, as I should have, I thought about how long I'll have to be in this group. I don't have a set date of discharge. My therapist and my doctor will decide if I'm ready to leave. That's a weird feeling, but I guess it's the same as it is in the hospital. You go home when the doctor says so. Of course you can demand to be discharged, but then you're going against medical advice, and I would worry that the insurance company might not pay.

When the lecture series was over, it was lunchtime. The front desk gave each of us a meal ticket for the cafeteria, which was nice because we could get anything we wanted. That's one thing I noticed about the hospital—they like to feed you well. I guess that helps calm patients down. But it makes it easy to gain weight, too.

Now it was time for the afternoon group sessions. The large group broke into three smaller groups for discussion. Each group had a therapist. I ended up with four young African American women patients. They were all from a poor part of town, and their problems varied from childhood abuse to problems with their boyfriends and trouble with their parents. They talked about problems that I had trouble relating to. Everyone was nice enough as I told my story about Bill, but I just didn't feel I fit in with this group.

Maybe I wouldn't really fit into any group. *How many people in this program were widowed because their husband had a work accident?* I asked myself. I couldn't imagine having to come to this program day after day. I was thrilled it was 3:00 in the afternoon—time to go home. All I wanted was to be alone with Lady. I didn't want to talk with anyone. I didn't want to see anyone. I just wanted to be with Lady.

Thursday, September 27, 2012

Before today's lecture began, I started to notice how people seemed to know each other. I wondered if they had been doing this for weeks, for months. Then I noticed one young woman I had met in the hospital. I didn't especially feel like talking with her, mostly because she was quite hyperactive, but all of a sudden she yelled hello to me from across the room. She started calling out to me, asking how I was doing. I felt embarrassed and decided I wasn't going to share my condition across the room. All I wanted was to sit quietly in my chair. But I felt I needed to acknowledge her greeting, so I asked how she was. Luckily, after a couple of minutes she found someone else she knew and started the process all over again. At least she was done with me.

Sitting there, staring into space, I saw Mary coming through the door. Now that was a person I was glad to see. I waved at her, and she sat down next to me. She didn't look very good. She was supposed to have been in the program yesterday, but she didn't show. She was still working with her lawyer, trying to get visitation rights with her daughter. She was broke and had to find a new place to live. Not a good story.

We sat through the lectures, and she decided she needed to go back into the hospital. I agreed with her. She was so shaky, so nervous. She left, heading toward the intake area, after being out for only two days. I felt like crying—I hoped the best for her.

Dr. Steven was at the door, calling my name. During our meeting I started crying, and I told him about Mary. I explained that we were all so fragile, so easily upset. I'm sure he already knew that. We talked a little more, and the session was over. I was sure he was watching my mood.

Friday, September 28, 2012

Only the third day of partial, and I want it to be over. My mind is thinking about what needs to be done at home. I've spent most of the summer and fall in the hospital.

My yard has become a pile of weeds. I have paperwork to go through. I feel so tired, but I'm not getting anything done. By the time I get home, I just sit on the couch, petting Lady and trying to find something to watch on TV.

What a life this is, I think to myself. At least the first couple of years after I lost Bill, I was doing more charitable activities. But now I'm sitting in this lecture program, feeling like I'm not accomplishing anything. *Is any of this really helping me?* I wonder. My mind wanders back to how much I want to die and be with Bill. I still pray for that every day.

Today I overheard a girl asking her therapist if she could skip coming to the program on Saturday. I was going to ask for that too. I checked with my therapist, and she said it was okay. Yay—two days off!

Saturday, September 29, 2012

So nice—I got to sleep in with Lady. I'll work on paperwork this afternoon. But I don't have the strength to think about doing yard work.

Sunday, September 30, 2012

I could finally go back to church. *Am I ready to face everyone?* I worried. It's been so long. I was told I had some visitors from church while I was in the hospital. Now that it was mentioned, I vaguely remembered seeing a couple of faces, but that was about it. I think they came during those few days that I was disoriented. I felt nervous about what they must think of me after all this time, but I decided to go.

Arriving at church, I got many hugs. People were delighted to see me. That was nice. At least I was back where I belonged. These people give me comfort. Mass started, and tears formed in my eyes with the first song. Songs are a strong reminder of Bill. He loved hearing all the old hymns, and he loved being the loudest singer in the group. Thank goodness he had a good voice.

I knew it was going to be difficult to go to the cemetery. I hadn't been able to go for a few weeks because of being in the hospital. I drove there with my nerves on edge, and I started crying as soon as I arrived. I didn't stay long.

After I got home, I spent a quiet afternoon with Lady. Luckily I found a father-son lawn service to cut my grass and dispose of my leaves. I am so thankful for that. But I knew I should get outside to clean up my plants, even though I didn't have much ambition for that either. I took Lady out, and soon I realized I didn't feel comfortable working outside. I got a knot in my stomach that wouldn't go away. It brought up more memories of working with Bill in the back yard.

Instead, I reminded myself I still had a table full of paperwork, including a lot of bills that I needed to get paid. I headed back inside with that excuse.

Monday, October 1, 2012

Partial just isn't suiting me well. The topics aren't what I want to hear. Today's topic was "Your Diet." Yes, I could be eating better, but I don't care about that. I just want to be with Bill. The next topic was "Addictions"—focusing on drug and alcohol. I don't crave alcohol. Yes, sometimes I self-medicate with alcohol, but not so much since my head injury from falling. I'm still worried if I drink too much it might affect my brain.

Tuesday, October 2, 2012

I used to love October. By now, Bill and I would have made our plans for our anniversary. Most often we would drive up north to Minocqua, where we had our honeymoon. It was so beautiful with all the fir trees. And it was just the two of us. Perfect.

But here I am in partial, and every day seems the same. Every day Dr. Steven meets with me, asking me questions. Watching me as I answer. I know I have many days to go.

Now I'm dreading October and heading into winter with nothing special planned. Knowing the cold is coming. Needing to keep the house closed up, the windows shut. I feel so alone. Even my good memories haunt me now. I get so tense that my chest and stomach feel like someone is gripping me.

Wednesday, October 3, 2012

One week in partial but it feels like two weeks. It's become more boring every day. I know it's me because I've heard that plenty of people like partial and say they got something out of it. I don't know if it's because my situation was different, or if I just don't like lectures—or both—but I'm not catching on to why this is so good. I've been careful not to show I don't like it, because I'm afraid I'd have to stay in the program longer.

Thursday, October 4, 2012

The afternoon groups aren't getting any better for me either. I don't want to hear all the stories these young girls are discussing. I feel sorry they had these problems, but they aren't mine, and I can't see how it's helping me. The therapist had me talk today, but I kept it short. I never have anything new to add, so there isn't much interest for the group.

Friday, October 5, 2012

I walked into the lecture area this morning, wondering if my therapist would let me skip Saturday again. I waited until the afternoon to ask her, and she said yes. Yay again! I'm starting to think you only have to come on Saturdays if they're afraid to leave you alone too long. I guess I passed that test.

Saturday, October 6, 2012

It feels so good to be home. I walked outside and looked around at my gardens in my yard. Everything is so overgrown. Old flowers should have been trimmed by now. Weeds should have been pulled. I tried working on a couple of beds, but my mind just wasn't into it. I came back inside the house. I'm going to skip it this year—it just seems like too much work.

Sunday, October 7, 2012

Going to church this week seemed easier, but going to the cemetery was harder. I don't understand why it's bothering me more than before. I got to our spot and sobbed. *What kind of life is left for me?* I asked God. I want so badly to be with Bill that I cried all the way home. And then I had a drink. And then another.

Monday, October 8, 2012

My ninth day in partial. I started looking around the room at other patients, checking on how many seemed to be listening and how many were taking naps, daydreaming, or talking to someone else. A couple of the therapists are pretty strict about not listening or distracting the class. But others just try to get through their lectures.

Tuesday, October 9, 2012

I think part of the problem I'm having is that I spent fifteen days inpatient before I came to partial. So this seems to be an extension of that two weeks. I've decided to try to listen to the lectures a little more carefully. At least I might get something out of them.

Wednesday, October 10, 2012

I realized I've been going at this all wrong. I need to prove to Dr. Steven that I'm getting better. So today in our session, I tried to seem more alert. I tried to explain to him that I'm trying harder to get exercise and paying more attention to my diet. I tried to say I was looking at activities I could do with others, to get me out of the house. He seemed impressed. I think…

Thursday, October 11, 2012

Today I asked Dr. Steven if he thought I was ready to end partial this week. He asked if I thought I was ready. So I had to go through an explanation convincing him I was ready. He also asked me if I had asked my therapist if I was ready. I told him I didn't know I was supposed to ask her, but that I would.

I talked to her this afternoon, and she asked me the same types of questions. I guess I passed, because she said she thought I was ready and that I should talk to my doctor the following day.

This is getting complicated.

Friday, October 12, 2012

As soon as Dr. Steven and I sat down today, I told him about my talk with my therapist. He agreed, saying that I was looking much better than when I started the program. They just needed to get my walking papers together, and I could go home. Thank goodness!

As I walked to my car, the last four months were whirling in my head. Since June, I had been admitted for seven days in the inpatient hospital, I had been in the four-week intensive outpatient program, again admitted for fifteen days in the inpatient hospital, and now had just completed the three- week partial hospital program. Wow—summing it up like that was mind-boggling.

I feel stronger now than I have in the last few months. All of this therapy has helped more than I gave it credit for. But I'm also nervous about being back on my own. Back to my isolation tactics. In two weeks I'll be facing our wedding anniversary. I know that will once again be difficult, so I'm glad I will again be seeing Gregg. But Dr. John is still gone. I need to call his administrative assistant to find out if she knows how long he'll be gone. And I need to schedule appointments to see Dr. Steven until Dr. John is back.

Friday, October 26, 2012

Today would have been our twenty-seventh wedding anniversary. When Bill and I were planning to stay home around our anniversary, we would ask our friends and relatives to stay away and try not to call unless they really needed us. We loved the privacy this gave us surrounding our big day. Now that Bill is gone, I still prefer it this way.

But today I had an appointment with Gregg. This I didn't mind because we would be talking about Bill, and I enjoy the talks that Gregg and I have. Today we talked about how I should spend the day. The first year I tried watching the video of our wedding, because that is what we always did. That was a big mistake. I wasn't ready for it, and I cried horribly. Gregg agreed it was best to put that off for a few years.

I told him I bought a bottle of champagne so I could drink it from both of our two wedding glasses. He wasn't so happy with that idea, but I decided to do it anyway. As it turned out later, Gregg was right. I felt so empty drinking alone on our day.

Last year I spent our anniversary in solitude, not even turning on the TV. That turned out to be a rough day. This year I felt the diversion of TV could be good. Maybe a movie—something not too sad and not too happy. I wanted to be careful to pick something that might keep me calmer. I didn't want any chance of going back into the hospital. Gregg agreed with that. He had hoped that this year I would let in a friend or family member as a diversion, but I wasn't ready for that.

I told him I was going to the cemetery after our appointment. He knew this was going to be hard on me, but he didn't give his opinion. He knew I was going either way. He was right again—I sobbed uncontrollably for quite some time.

Tonight was a difficult evening, but it helped that I saw Gregg today. Facing bedtime was another huge struggle. Back came the sobbing.

Wednesday, October 31, 2012

It's been difficult not seeing Dr. John weekly. I set up a couple of appointments with Dr. Steven, but he'll only see me every three weeks. I'm surprised that, after all that time in the hospital and the outpatient programs, he won't see me more often. But he said that's the way he does it. I'm not going to argue, but it has been difficult.

Friday, November 2, 2012

Gregg reminded me again to make a list of my weekly activities. Before I was hospitalized, I was instructed to do this by both Dr. John and Gregg. They wanted to keep track of my activities to check if I was isolating myself again. Now I need to start again.

I'll see Carla on Mondays, and Gregg said I have to attend a weekly mental health group at the hospital on Tuesdays. I have Bible study on Wednesdays, I cook for Fr. Sam and his mom on Thursdays, I see Gregg on Fridays, I'm hoping to see Beth on Saturdays, and I have church on Sundays.

I also occasionally go to Roger's house. I didn't see him much this summer and fall, so it's good to be back to my old schedule.

They are all trying to keep me out of the hospital. So am I.

Tuesday, November 6, 2012

Today was my first session with the mental health group, and I was nervous again. I walked in only to find that the therapist was Julie, from the inpatient groups. I was glad because I was used to her. There were about eight people in the group, similar to the inpatient groups.

During the session, they went around the table and Julie asked each person to give a brief summary of how the last week went for them—good or bad. I felt uncomfortable, once again needing to explain my circumstances. And since I was new, I didn't know any of the other participants, so I also didn't know much about why they were there. Maybe some detective work would be helpful.

I gave a short history of my problems and then let the others talk.

Thursday, November 8, 2012

During my hospital stay, I was also encouraged to find a grief group. After searching for a while, I found one that met at a church. I called the group coordinator, Kathy, and she let me know the group meets on Thursdays, and that I could come to tonight's meeting. Now I feel scared again.

With hopes high, I walked into the grief group for the first time tonight. The room held a small group of people, all with different losses. One couple lost their teenage daughter, one woman lost her mother, one man lost his wife, and one couple was there because the man had lost his first wife, and he had children still missing their mother.

Everyone was nice, but I didn't feel instantly comfortable in this group. Nevertheless I'm determined to give it a try and continue to go to the meetings.

Monday, November 12, 2012

Today I had a session with Carla. I hadn't seen her for a long time, so I was a bit nervous. She told me we would be having a therapy appointment because I wasn't stable enough to go through with PTSD treatments. That sounded accurate to me, and we just talked.

Wednesday, November 14, 2012

I've missed Dr. John's Wednesday talks. I've been wondering how he's doing. I've also missed being able to get a solid night's sleep. Since Dr. Steven cut my medication, my nights often have been a nightmare.

Thursday, November 15, 2012

My second grief group session. Same people. Each session has a different topic, and today's topic was, "How to get through the holidays." Basically no one was happy about the holidays arriving soon. We won't be meeting next week due to Thanksgiving. The following week we'll be discussing how we did over this holiday.

Wednesday, November 21, 2012

My birthday. I wish I could just skip it. I spent the afternoon making pies for tomorrow's Thanksgiving dinner. It's so painful to make these pies, knowing just how much Bill loved them.

This evening Beth, her husband Gary, their daughter Rebecca, and Rebecca's fiancé Jim came over to celebrate my birthday. It was nice having them all over to my house. The evening started out very nice, but it went downhill when I asked Gary and Beth if they would help me pick out a Christmas tree. I wanted to make it as short as possible. But Gary put his foot down, saying I was going to join their family on Saturday to cut a tree.

My heart stopped.

This was a tradition that Bill and I had created with our kids. Thanksgiving weekend was full of preparations for Christmas. Thursday, of course, we ate our big meal with the family. Friday we would go to Clifford's restaurant for a fish fry, and Saturday we spent picking out a tree with my friend Beth's family and the other Kaiserling family.

Bill's brother Scott, his wife Debbie, their kids, and Beth's family would all meet at our house and we would caravan to a tree lot. Bill would bring his chain saw and, with a big smile, he would help other families cut their trees down. After bringing our trees home, all three families would help put our tree up, and we girls would pull out all the Thanksgiving leftovers, heat them up, and we would have another large meal for everyone.

Sunday and Monday were spent decorating the tree and house for Christmas. This time of year held such wonderful memories. Memories I had difficulty thinking about. And sadly, I vowed I would never do these activities again without Bill. They were filled with too much pain.

But Gary insisted I was coming. They would be showing up at my house to bring me along. After a lot of tears, I hesitantly agreed to go.

Thursday, November 22, 2012—Thanksgiving

I think the worst part of the day now is getting up early to prepare the turkey and dressing before putting them in the oven. Mom and I did this project for years. And when Mom passed away, Bill got out of bed and filled in as a helper. It was so sweet of him, and it made it much more enjoyable. So now doing it alone is painful.

The meal itself was easier when the family showed up to help, but I had to hold in the hurt of Bill not being part of the group anymore. And now I no longer want to have leftovers in the house because that also reminds me of all the meals I would make for Bill and me.

By the end of the day, I gave everyone something to take home. But as I worked on putting the dishes in the dishwasher, I kept picturing Bill making his turkey sandwiches for the next few days.

Friday, November 23, 2012

I was exhausted from yesterday's activities, but I had my session with Gregg to get to. He wanted to know how I did, getting through the holiday. He knew these days were hard on me. And then I told him about going with my friends to get a Christmas tree tomorrow. When I explained why I was dreading it, he understood and was sympathetic. He reminded me I could say no, but I told him they would show up anyway.

I spent the remainder of today resting at home. I needed some time alone, to think about Bill. But I'm also thinking about going tree hunting tomorrow, and that's keeping me very tense.

Saturday, November 24, 2012

I got up, got Lady settled, and waited for Beth's family to arrive. Over and over my thoughts were of Bill, picturing him gathering what he needed for the trip—checking the chainsaw, grabbing rags for marking possible trees, hooking up the trailer to the car. Soon Beth's family drove up, and we headed to the tree lot. Beth assured me that they had found a new lot, so it wasn't one that we had visited with Bill.

Wrong.

When we arrived at the lot, I soon realized that I had found this lot before, and Bill had been with us. I went into a sort of shock, walking around and just staring at the ground. Very sweetly, Rebecca, my godchild, held my arm as I walked up and down trying to find a tree. Each time I passed a tree stump, I wondered if it was one that Bill had cut with his chain saw.

Beth's family all seemed to be trying their best to divert my attention. That was good, since I was having difficulty holding myself together. Luckily we picked out our trees pretty fast, and the task was over.

Back at home, Beth's family helped me put up the tree. I decided I would let it stay there undecorated until sometime closer to Christmas. Happily, we all went to a Mexican restaurant for lunch. That was a good break from my memories of heating up leftovers. I tried to relax, because I knew they were attempting to make new memories for me, trying to ease my pain.

Thursday, November 29, 2012

My third grief group. We sat in a circle and discussed how we did over the holiday. I expected everyone probably had a hard time, like I did. Wrong. Most didn't have a great time, but they were surprised how well they did. Now I was really feeling separated from the group. I wasn't comfortable, and I felt I should watch what I said.

Afterward I talked with the coordinator, Kathy. She seemed to understand my discomfort and told me they have a short video on missing your spouse. She'll bring it to the next session, and I can watch it while the group talks about other things.

Thursday, December 6, 2012

My fourth grief group. One more try. When I got to the session, Kathy had the video for me. I played it and immediately knew I wasn't going to continue with the grief group.

First of all, the video was narrated by a married couple. Each had been previously widowed. That immediately brought an uncomfortable feeling to me. As the video continued, they did include a short section on grief and loss. But then they started talking about having a new life, and dating—so unlike what I was experiencing. I felt so disappointed with the video that I gave up.

I explained to Kathy that I was going to leave the group. She said she was sad to see me go, and she suggested I try a monthly widows' group that also meets at Elm Grove Church. The group is Christian-based and uses the scriptures as part of the meeting. The suggestion is great—I wish she had told me sooner. Kathy is going to email me the phone number of the coordinators for that group.

Friday, December 7, 2012

After receiving an email from Kathy, I found out the next widows' group meeting is tomorrow. What good timing! I'm very interested in attending.

Saturday, December 8, 2012

As I walked through the hallways leading to the widows' group meeting room, I felt my anxiety growing. *What if this group also isn't a fit for me?* I wondered. But as I entered the room and looked at the faces, I felt a sense of relief. Instantly, I knew everyone had gone through the same type of experience that I had. Maybe the details were different, but the endings were all the same: we had all lost our husbands.

It was a friendly group, with women stopping to say hello to me. They told me they were glad I came, and that made me feel welcome. We all introduced ourselves, and stated how long it had been since we became widows. Normally I don't like this type of drill, but this time it was different. I felt like I knew each woman intimately. I knew I would want to treat each of these women as God's fragile creatures. Sure, some of these women were strong, juggling careers and families. But they carried a grief inside themselves that only another widow could understand.

After talking for a while, we broke into groups to read a passage of scripture and then analyze it. There are many scriptures in the Bible that pertain to widows—God also knew the care we need. It was all a comfort to me, and I knew I would be returning.

After the meeting ended, Rosemary came up to me to say hi. She was one of four leaders of the group, and she was checking to see how I was doing. We talked, and I instantly enjoyed her company. She asked if I would like to meet for coffee sometime, and I agreed—that would be nice.

I knew I finally had found a group that I liked. Walking back to my car, I felt a peace that I had seldom felt since losing Bill.

Thursday, December 13, 2012

Today is Bill's birthday. I made plans to meet Rosemary for coffee, knowing this would be a good diversion for me. I sensed that her company would bring me comfort.

We began to talk as if we had known each other for years. She shared her story of loss with me, and I explained my story of loss to her. She had been widowed for twelve years, so she could tell me how her feelings had evolved through the years. She told me she still misses her husband every day, but her emotions have settled down some. I told her I was writing a book about my life with Bill, and what the loss has done to me. She immediately asked if she could read it, and I promised to send her an electronic copy.

We decided to meet every couple of weeks. What a nice beginning of a friendship.

Mid-December 2012

Beth went with me to shop for Christmas presents. She has been my favorite person to shop with since childhood. And I knew she'd be a great help coming up with ideas for presents. I was tense while we shopped, but when we were finished, I was glad most of it was done.

Scott, Deb, and the kids came over to help me decorate the Christmas tree. We all worked on getting the lights on the tree, and then the kids put up the ornaments. David was a big help putting together the Christmas village.

After they all left, I stared at the tree. I used to love looking at our Christmas tree. Now I was sinking deep into my memories of Bill again. And they were difficult.

Friday, December 21, 2012

At my session with Gregg today, I broke down crying. I told him that my tension is increasing as Christmas draws closer. I'm thinking about Bill all the time, and it's terribly depressing not having him here during the holidays. I've been talking about ending things again, and Gregg wondered if I should go back into the hospital. I told him no, I couldn't disappoint everyone by not having Christmas Eve at my house.

He reminded me that I need to keep safe for myself. I didn't have an answer to that.

Saturday, December 22, 2012

Our friends Bob and Gail are down from Northern Wisconsin for the week. Bill and I used to visit their lake cottage about once a year; those were wonderful trips. Today I had lunch at a Mexican restaurant with them and with Pat and Jenni. Bob and Pat are good friends of Bill's from work, and I love the company of Gail and Jenni. I don't get to see them often, so it was great having lunch together.

They asked how my summer was, so it was time to explain that I had been in the hospital twice and that the holidays were causing me some tension. I knew they were disappointed to hear that. They wished the best for me, and I guess they had hoped I had found a way to grieve less. But I still treasured the time with them.

Monday, December 24, 2012 — Christmas Eve

The family is here for Christmas Eve. I'm feeling tense, but I'm glad the family still wants to come to my house, as we always did when Bill was here. After dinner, Scott hooked up my computer with Skype so we were able to see my stepson Billy, his wife, Heidi, and the kids on a computer screen. Billy took me on a tour of his new house in Texas. This technology is amazing. And it was great to see Billy and his family without having to travel. I'm glad they're happy in Texas, but I miss them.

Tuesday, December 25, 2012—Christmas Day

I wished for a quiet day and I got it. I still prefer isolation, but then memories of Bill drift in and I get very tense with a knot in my stomach. I wish I could think of Bill without getting so anxious.

Roger came over this evening; that helped. I let him know just how shaky I had been feeling and that my fill-in psychiatrist (Dr. Steven) and my therapist (Gregg) wanted me to go into the hospital. I agreed—I knew I needed to go.

Roger stayed for a nice long time. I knew he was trying to help me. I told him I could go to the hospital by myself the next day because I had an appointment with Dr. Steven, and he would admit me. I had been told I could park my car in the usual parking lot and keep it there until I was discharged. I thought Roger would take Lady with him, but he said she would be good company for me tonight, and he was right. Roger said he would pick Lady up tomorrow. He was so sweet.

After he left I nervously packed a few things to be ready for tomorrow. I am dreading going into the hospital, but I know I need to do it. Lady crawled into bed with me, and I'm so glad she's here. I know I'll be missing her again.

Wednesday, December 26, 2012 — Third inpatient stay

As I left the house to go to my appointment with Dr. Steven, I felt terrible being separated from Lady again. At least she enjoys being at Roger's house with all of his pets.

I drove to the hospital, thinking about how this was the third time I was being admitted this year. I felt like I was getting worse. The holidays were too much for me.

I arrived for my appointment with Dr. Steven and told him I was ready to go into the hospital. He agreed, and he walked me over to intake. After the usual registration process, I was admitted.

Much to my disappointment, I discovered I'd been admitted to a different unit than the last two times. That made me nervous. But luckily, some of the staff I had met during my previous admissions were also in this unit, and that helped.

Going through the process of being admitted for the third time felt like a familiar routine. I was thinking about the first time I was admitted, when this process was so scary. Today I went through the motions, while the hospital staff checked me and my bag to make sure I didn't have anything not allowed in the hospital and locked up what they needed to keep, such as my purse and cell phone. After receiving my medications, I was ready for sleep.

Thursday, December 27, 2012 — Inpatient hospitalization

My first full day in the hospital today, like the other times, was filled with visits from nurses, the therapist, the medical doctor, a nutritionist, my case worker, and my psychiatrist. I quickly found out that being admitted into the hospital during the holiday week meant staff were taking vacation days. Even though I was admitted by Dr. Steven, he was now on vacation, so I was being seen by the psychiatrist on call. Again, a new psychiatrist—and again, that made me nervous. I felt like we were starting from scratch again.

The on-call psychiatrist gave me his opinion of my situation. He was right in many ways, but he didn't know me, and I wasn't happy with this situation. He said he was going to take a look at my medications to see if any adjustments should be made. I instantly became scared, remembering how badly things had gone after my medications were changed during my last hospitalization. *Here we go again,* I thought.

I was on edge most of the day. Everything on this unit seems so different. I stayed by myself as usual, trying to get through the day, although this afternoon I went to a group session.

When I received my evening medications, it seemed that they had been cut back some again. I'm not looking forward to trying to sleep.

Friday, December 28, 2012

Last night I had trouble sleeping. I was right—the psychiatrist on call had changed something. I so miss Dr. John being my doctor, and I pray he will be returning soon.

Today I knew I was to attend all four of the group therapy sessions. And I wanted to attend. Hearing the various stories of all the patients somehow left me feeling a bit calmer, and helped me know the patients better. But I'm tired and tense because of the medication changes.

Again, I stayed by myself as much as possible. I haven't found anyone else I feel comfortable with. This time I brought one of my own books to read, so I spent most of my free time in my room. I feel awfully lonely here, and I know I shouldn't be isolating.

Tonight, as I lay in bed, I watched the nurses' aide doing her rounds. She checked in on me every fifteen minutes, making sure I was okay, until I finally fell asleep. Obviously I'm not sleeping well. So much for the medication changes.

Saturday, December 29, 2012

Same routine: group sessions, nurses and nurses' aides talking with me. I'm not clicking with this group as well as in the other unit. Most of the patients are very quiet, as I am. There is very little eye contact with each other.

I continued to stay in my room today; I told the on-call psychiatrist that I've had trouble getting to sleep. I didn't get much of a response to that. It reminds me of the responses I didn't get from Dr. Steven.

Tonight, as I lay awake in bed, I heard a commotion down by the nurses' desk. A patient was yelling at the nurses to let him go home. It was late at night, so the nurses were trying to calm him down. But he was way past calming down. He was demanding his belongings and wanted to go home. He was either pounding on the desk or kicking it. Either way, it was loud, and I was becoming quite tense. I knew it didn't involve me, but I was growing anxious nevertheless. And to add to that, my room was just across the hallway from the locked exit door.

The hospital patrolmen came in to help with the situation. The whole event was very noisy, with the patrolmen opening that door and walking down the hallway, and then more loud voices as the patrolmen and the patient argued. Finally, the noise quieted down. I was curious how it had been resolved, but I knew I wouldn't find out.

Even after it was over, I stayed very tense. The nursing assistant kept checking on me. She knew I was awake, but nothing was being done about it.

Finally I decided to ask my nurse if there was any medication I could take. Usually the nurses are quite caring and helpful, but the nurse I had that night wasn't. He said I'd had plenty of medications already. I went back to my room feeling angry and frightened. I knew I was going to have trouble getting any sleep. I resigned myself to watching the nursing assistant do her rounds, over and over.

Sunday, December 30, 2012

I was extremely tired today after not getting much sleep last night. I decided to talk to my day nurse about what happened. I wanted to tell somebody that I didn't want that same evening nurse again because he had upset and frightened me. The day nurse listened carefully, and she told me she would talk with someone about the possibility of a change. I felt better that I had talked with someone.

Once again, I was being seen by a different psychiatrist. This was the doctor covering the holiday weekend. He seemed nice, but it was unnerving to once again have someone new. I briefly explained my situation and the problems I was having with tension and getting to sleep. Thank goodness, he increased my medications again.

Tonight I was assigned to a different night nurse; I'm glad for that. But as I sat in the TV room, the nurse from last night came to talk with me. I really didn't feel like doing that, but he asked me what he had done wrong. I tried to explain how the noise from the patient yelling had upset me, and I needed something to calm me down or get me to sleep. And if he couldn't do that, maybe he could have just talked with me for a while. He apologized, but I still didn't think he got it. I was glad I had a new nurse.

Monday, December 31, 2012—New Year's Eve

Today I'm facing New Year's Eve with the same routine—group sessions, nurses talking with me, and my session with the psychiatrist. Not the same as at home.

The unit is getting more crowded, and it's filling up with patients who have more noticeable mental illnesses. I learned that the county hospital is full, so they've been bringing some patients from there. As a result, the unit was too crowded and noisy for me today; I felt my tension increasing. The staff is so busy with these new patients that they don't have time for everyone. I tried to stay in my room when I could and deal with my anxiety.

During a group session, the therapist suggested that she put some soothing music on. I asked that she not do that because I wasn't able to listen to any music without getting anxious. She was nice and said she wouldn't do it then. After the session was done, she explained that another therapist will be handling the next session. One of the patients knew who this was and told me this therapist always plays music during the session. I told her I would ask that she not play any, and if she insisted, I would leave.

That is exactly what happened. The therapist came in explaining that she was going to play some music, and I let her know that listening to any music upsets me. She just went ahead and put the CD in her player, saying it would be good for everyone.

I became emotional and started crying, picked up my materials, and headed for my room. When I got there, I was so upset that I started sobbing. The therapist must have told the staff, because a nurse came in to talk with me. I calmed down somewhat, but here I was again—in my room, not wanting to be with anyone.

My memories turned to past New Year's Eves. Bill had planned a special New Year's Eve to start 1985 by asking me to marry him. We had joined up with Dave and Jaci, our special friends. They were having a large New Year's celebration at the Eagles Club, an old but beautiful building on the main road downtown, called Wisconsin Ave. It was also special because my parents had met there just after WWII. There was a dinner and two bands playing for us—a Beatles-type band and another band that we had seen before and enjoyed.

Bill had planned to ask me on the dance floor right at midnight, but I managed to ruin his surprise. Two weeks earlier I had started asking Bill about our relationship, and he had answered in a way that made me think he didn't want to consider it. I got upset, and he knew I was going to stay upset over Christmas, so he asked me then. That too was very romantic, but I felt bad when I later heard what he was originally planning to do. It all worked out okay—we were engaged and he still did it in a loving way.

Tuesday, January 1, 2013 — New Year's Day

Another New Year, and here I was—still in a psychiatric facility.

I saw the new psychiatrist on call. He increased another medication today. I think I'm back where I started again.

He wanted to know more of my history with losing Bill, and we had a long talk. He was clearly interested in my story. He explained that he does research papers on this subject, so that probably explained why he talked to me for so long. And that was fine with me.

At the end of the session, he said I could go home today. I felt like saying, "Thank goodness!" but then the next moment I was nervous about leaving the hospital. That same thing has happened each time I am discharged. Part of me wants to get out and continue my own life, but part of me feels scared because I won't have someone watching me all day, every day.

After being discharged, I drove to Roger's house to get Lady. Seeing how excited she was to see me sure made me feel good. I didn't stay long because I wanted to get home before dark. Going home was also made easier because Lady was with me, and I knew she'd be in bed with me tonight.

I felt exhausted, and I thought how strange it was—one minute in the hospital, and the next minute at home. Now I'm worried how I'll do this coming week.

Wednesday, January 2, 2013

I've been feeling fragile. I must gain enough strength to handle living alone again. And I need to make some plans to do something that will make me feel useful. My therapy team will be making sure I'm doing something every day, but right now I'm back to isolating in my own house. And that's an awfully lonely feeling.

Friday, January 4, 2013

In my session with Gregg today, I was right: one of his first comments was asking for a list of what I do every day. I told him that I was thinking of trying to get Lady certified to be a therapy dog. He loved that idea. He knows how much she means to me, and it would get me out of the house to be with other people. I promised Gregg that I would check online to see if there were any local dog trainers.

Thursday, January 10, 2013

I found a dog trainer in my area, and today I took Lady to the first day of a six-week therapy dog training class. After this class, we'll need to go before a testing board to get her certified. I was nervous going in, but Lady surprised me—she followed most of my instructions. The problem is that she gets too excited around the other dogs. The instructor says the testing board won't approve any growling or aggressive behavior, so we might be in trouble. The other problem is her age. Halfway through the exercises she lies down, looking tired. This is going to be a challenge.

Tuesday, January 22, 2013

I met Rosemary today for coffee and conversation. We hadn't been able to meet since before the holidays, so it was good to see her again. In the twelve years that she has been a widow, it's amazing how much she has been through that is similar to my experiences. We both enjoyed getting together, and we decided to meet every couple of weeks.

Monday, January 28, 2013

Finally—Dr. John is back! Today was my first appointment with him in four months. It calmed me immensely, He looks much better now, and I'm so glad for his return. I've missed the stability he gives me.

Sunday, February 3, 2013

Today is the first service with our new Anglican priest, Fr. Patrick. Everyone, including me, seems to like him very much. And this time, we're getting more than a priest. We are also getting his family: a wife and three grown children. Father has already moved here from Ohio, but the rest of the family will need to wait until June, when the youngest son graduates from his high school class in Ohio. Then they'll be looking for a place to live. They all seem nice, so I hope it works out.

Friday, February 15, 2013

Today is "Key's Day"—as Bill put it, the anniversary he created to show he was romantic even without the card companies telling him to do so on the 14th. We had such fun on these anniversaries, going out to dinner, having a romantic evening afterward. Unfortunately, it's another memory that brings sadness to me, now that I'm alone.

Tuesday, March 5, 2013

I've returned to the weekly mental health group on Tuesdays. It's part of my goal to participate in an activity every day. I still don't like going to these sessions, but the faces are becoming familiar now, so it's a little bit easier.

Wednesday, March 6, 2013

Bible study has begun at my house again. We meet twice a week: Wednesday mornings with a light snack, and Thursday evenings with a light dinner. I enjoy learning as much as I can about God's word, and Fr. Pat does a great job explaining scripture to us. I feel very peaceful during these sessions.

It's been such a blessing to have Fr. Pat and his family join our Holy Cross Anglican Church. In a short time, Fr. Pat has brought more peace to our congregation.

Thursday, March 7, 2013

I have become fast friends with Rosemary. She understands my situation more than anyone I have found. She says her pain isn't as sharp as it used to be, or as painful as I am experiencing now, but it still hurts. We've decided that there are a lot more widows and widowers in pain than people realize. It's sad, but it gives me comfort to know I share this grief with others.

Mid-March 2013

Day after day, I continue to feel the need to stop my suffering. I drink some to ease the pain, but that doesn't help much anymore. I feel empty, waiting and hoping for my turn to go to Heaven. I want God to fill my void. And, then, hopefully, I'll also be with Bill.

Thank goodness Dr. John is back. It's so helpful talking to him. I can tell him everything. But now I won't be able to see Gregg, my therapist, much longer because his credentials don't qualify for Medicare insurance payments. I'm so disappointed— he's been a strong support system for me, and I've loved our conversations. He's looking for another therapist who I can see instead.

All of these changes are very unnerving to me. I just got Dr. John back, and now I feel like I'm experiencing a new loss. I'm quite anxious and having trouble sleeping again.

Thursday, March 21, 2013

I had coffee with Rosemary today. She lifts my spirits. Just one visit and we became friends. I'm able to tell her how I'm doing without feeling judged. I feel bad, though, because when I tell her how I'm doing, she worries.

Monday, March 25, 2013

My psychiatrist and therapists have decided I should attend therapy group sessions called "Dialectical Behavioral Therapy" (DBT). It's a program that deals with living in the present. And being aware of your emotions enough to take note of them, and then being able to set them aside. It sounds like a long shot for me, but I guess I'll be going.

Today was the first orientation meeting. A DPT therapist, Diana, leads the four orientation meetings. As usual, I felt uncomfortable in this new group, but I did like Diana. She mentioned that it was good to have a DPT therapist if you're going to DPT classes. I liked that idea, so I decided that it was time to switch therapists. Instead of seeing Carla, I'm going to see Diana weekly. Since Diana is schooled in DPT therapy, I figured it was a better fit. If I'm stronger at a later time, I'll return to Carla to work on PTSD.

March 28, 2013

Barbara, a woman from church, volunteers at the VA Hospital in town. She told me that the veterans could use presents. Simple things they could use every day, like socks, combs, toothbrushes, toothpaste, paper, pens, envelopes, and stamps. I decided on socks. Beth helped me buy a cartload of socks to go into individual clear bags we got. We marked each bag with a "Thank you." I went to the VA today to disperse the gifts of socks to the patients.

Wednesday, May 1, 2013

Today was my first day in a DBT group session. I've been dreading this. I don't like group sessions. I get very nervous, and I have a hard time relating to what others are saying about their situations. Mine seems so different.

There are about ten people in the group, and my new therapist, Diana, leads it. I just sat and listened, trying to learn about the group members. I came home feeling quite anxious and not wanting to continue with this group. But I know I have to give it a try.

Tuesday, May 7, 2013

Today is the last therapy dog training session for Lady. She passed the course, so next I need to get her certified. That will be the hard part. I also had to take an online handler course to prove I knew all the rules for taking a therapy dog into a facility. I aced that part, so now it's Lady's turn.

Saturday, May 11, 2013

Today is Julie's baby shower. The youngest of Bill's three kids, she got married a couple of years ago, and I expected they would want to start a family. Beth and I drove together to her house, and thank goodness, Beth printed a map, because I never saw so many twists and turns to get to a house. They just bought it and moved in a while back, so I was glad her shower was at her house so I could see it.

I was nervous about going to a social event, as I don't do well with a lot of people all talking about their lives. But it worked out pretty well. I was focused enough on sitting with Beth and with Debbie, my sister-in-law, that I stayed quite calm.

Friday, May 17, 2013

My last session with my therapist, Gregg, was today, and I'm brokenhearted. I've been seeing him for three years, and our conversations have been incredibly helpful. I cried during most of the session. I even saw tears in Gregg's eyes. What a sad day.

Monday, May 20, 2013

Beth has been very busy lately, so we haven't been able to see each other much. Her mom is sick, and Beth and her husband Gary are taking her into their home. I understand how much work this is, because Bill and I took my parents into our house. You know it's the best thing to do, but it changes your life completely.

Thank goodness for emails—at least we can stay in touch. I like receiving and sending these short messages. They keep me in contact with others. I also get emails from my friend Susan. Years back we worked together, but we've kept in touch. I enjoy that.

Susan has been suffering her own loss: the death of her sister. Susan and her sister lived together for many years and enjoyed life together. Even though it's different from losing a husband, for her, it's a deeply felt, difficult loss.

Wednesday, May 22, 2013

Bible study is continuing at my house, thanks to Fr. Pat. It's a small group from church, and Fr. Pat does a wonderful job of picking scriptures and explaining them to us. I look forward to it each week.

Thursday, May 23, 2013

As I walk around my yard, all I see are weeds and overgrown plants, including a large amount of buckthorns— an invasive bush that grows very fast and has needle-like thorns all over the branches. The buckthorns kill whatever is in their way and are almost impossible to kill themselves. So I at least try to keep them smaller.

I've done very little yard work during the last couple of years, and it shows. I started weeding some but realized I would need to do more than this. And help came. During my DBT group sessions, there were fliers on the table from a woman named Nancy, stating she was for hire for quite a few tasks, including yard work. I decided to give her a call. She sounded nice, and she seemed knowledgeable, so I asked her to come over and give it a try. After working a couple of times, she suggested I get a load of mulch. We could lay newspaper over the weeds first, and then top them with a thick layer of mulch. I liked the idea and started checking on places that sell mulch. I found the one I wanted, and asked them to deliver a truck full of mulch.

The day it arrived, I was shocked—I got what I asked for. A huge dump truck pulled into my driveway and dumped the load onto an area that already had mulch on it. As they were dumping the load, I stared in shock at the size of the mountain I had bought. It was huge. But I had a feeling I would use all of it.

Nancy helped spread some of it, but that was the last day she ever showed up for work. I guess she didn't like that job. So it became my job and I worked on it until fall. I left the rest of the mountain until next spring.

Friday, May 24, 2013

Today was my first session with my new therapist, Ken. I'm horrible with changes, so I've been apprehensive about it. I deeply miss my therapist Gregg; it's going to be hard to replace him.

Our first session was different from what I expected. Ken seemed to know quite a bit about me, which is no surprise. I'm guessing he read my file and had conversations with Gregg. And he talked mostly about himself during the session. I guess he felt I would be more comfortable hearing about him, but if it continues I'll need to let him know I can't hear about families and couples. There's too much hurt in that topic for me.

I left the session with Ken feeling worried, but I'll continue to give him a try. He seems like a nice man, and I don't want to be too hasty. And I am fast approaching the anniversary of the day I met Bill. I'm already feeling quite tense.

Memorial Day Weekend 2013

I'm extremely depressed and alone in my house. I'm thinking about the anniversary of meeting Bill, and I don't feel like doing much else. The anniversary is this coming Tuesday, but originally, in 1982, it was on a Friday. I'm crying quite a lot, trapped in my living room lounge chair, staring off into space, with my thoughts all over the place. Each time I become a little more alert, I again start thinking about Bill.

I'm feeling a desperate need to get to Bill. *Could I, would I go ahead and do it?* I ask myself. *What would God decide about me?* I have many questions in my head.

I had a few drinks, partially to block out the pain, but mostly to turn down my inhibitions so I could do what I had to do to get to Bill. But I didn't go through with it.

Tuesday, May 28, 2013

Thirty-one years ago I met Bill. Once again I went over the story of our first night in my head. Sometimes I can get pretty far before the bad memories cloud the good ones and I have to concentrate on something else.

Now I realize that strolling down Memory Lane wasn't a good idea, because I'm starting to have thoughts about Bill's accident and his absence. That's when memories lead to heartache. And worse, I start thinking of ways to be with Bill.

Today I felt a strong sense of panic, like I was drowning in my depression. I checked my phone messages; I had a message from Rosemary, my widow friend. I decided to return her call. She would understand what I was going through. Rosemary answered, and I explained what was going on. She sounded worried about what I might do, and she tried to get me to promise I wouldn't do anything to harm myself. She said if I refused to promise to be safe, she would call someone—the police, Fr. Patrick, or Dr. John.

When she continued to press me for an answer, I finally promised not to do anything. She insisted I give her the phone numbers for Fr. Patrick and Dr. John anyway. She was going to call me later, and if I didn't answer, she would call one or both of these two numbers. I felt horrible that I was scaring her, but I was so deep in my depression that it made it too hard to say I was okay.

About a half hour after we hung up, Fr. Patrick called me. Of course I thought Rosemary had called him, so I started the conversation with him explaining what was going on. He didn't have a clue what I was talking about. He was calling to let me know Bible study was cancelled the next morning. I was glad about that, but then he started to ask me what was going on. I explained, and he also grew concerned. He wouldn't hang up until I promised I wouldn't hurt myself.

Wow! I felt that God was intervening to get me to settle down. After I finally promised Fr. Patrick that I wouldn't do anything to harm myself, we hung up. Shortly thereafter, Rosemary called back to see if I was still okay. I said that I was and that Fr. Pat had coincidently called and now knew what was going on. I let her know that I was getting tired and would be going to bed.

I fell asleep just amazed by what good friends I had, and how close God was to me.

Wednesday, May 29, 2013

I held my emotions in check pretty well during the day, but while driving to my appointment with Dr. John, I knew they were starting to surface. As had happened so often before, I had a compulsion to go home, get out the bottle of Southern Comfort, and try to block out the pain. This time the urge to end it all was pushing me hard. I knew I had to talk to Dr. John about it.

At the beginning of our appointment, I burst into tears and told Dr. John what was going on. He tried to settle me down, but I continued crying and telling him how desperate I felt. He gave me three choices: 1) I could be admitted to the hospital, 2) I could go home and he would call the police to check on me later, or 3) I could promise not to do anything harmful that night, call Fr. Patrick, and then call him next.

I sat there for a while, undecided. Finally Dr. John got firmer with me to choose one or be sent to the hospital. I finally agreed that I wouldn't do anything harmful, and I went home. I wasn't sure if I believed my own promise, though—and I'm sure Dr. John was thinking the same thing. I couldn't have felt more depressed.

I called Fr. Pat and explained the story to him. Before I knew it, he and his wife, Robin, were at my front door, and we had a long talk this evening. Some of what Fr. Pat had to say was hard for me to hear. And he was quoting scripture to me—I didn't have a chance of arguing with that.

After they left, I called Dr. John. He made sure I was all right and told me to call him again tomorrow. Hearing his voice helped calm me down. I told him I was exhausted and was going to bed. He said he was happy about that.

Thursday, May 30, 2013

I again called Dr. John, and he asked me for Fr. Pat's number, because Fr. Pat had called him. It was a weird feeling, knowing my psychiatrist and my priest were having a conversation about me. But it was also a good feeling, knowing I had two such wonderful people watching out for me.

Tonight was Bible study night. I didn't feel up to it, but since it's at my house, I didn't want to cancel it. As everyone was arriving, I felt quite tense. My mind was on Bill, and I was having a hard time coping. Fr. Pat arrived and gave me a sweet hello. That helped. I knew once we got started with the Bible reading, I would feel more comfortable. And that came true. I calmed down a little more, although Bill was still in my thoughts.

As we were wrapping up the study, I couldn't help thinking about the difference between being in my house with church friends and being in the hospital. During the social time it was difficult to put on a happy face and try to look okay. Maybe I should have taken Dr. John's suggestion about going into the hospital. Everyone knows I've been in the hospital before; it wouldn't be much of a secret anymore. But it still embarrasses me.

Most people think you should be over grieving in a year or less. It's hard to hear the comments from well-meaning friends saying Bill is still with me, I should get on with my life, and would Bill want me to be like this? I can logically answer all these questions, but my heart and soul can't get to that point. I know Bill is gone from this world, to a better place. I'm not trying to get Bill back. But I'm trying to get myself to where Bill is.

Friday, May 31, 2013

Today was my second session with my new therapist, Ken. I'm not sure what to think yet. I need to stop comparing him to Gregg. He does a lot of generalized talking, so I have tried to interrupt and talk about how I'm feeling. It still feels awkward. But I can tell he is starting to listen to me, because he'll bring up things I've previously said. And I think he talked with Dr. John, because he's also suggesting that I go into the hospital again.

I'm still hedging on that topic.

Wednesday, June 5, 2013

I received a call from my first choice for a publisher, Brighton Publishing. They let me know they're interested in my book about my life with Bill, and I'm so excited—I can't believe my book is being accepted after my first attempt at writing. My goal of making Bill's memory permanent, and of helping other widows, is actually happening. It's amazing.

I let Dr. John know about the book at our session. He was thrilled and said he wants a signed copy. He's happy whenever I focus on something positive, instead of wishing for a short life. I'm not sure I can always do that.

Thursday, June 6, 2013

I'm starting to hear Summerfest commercials, naming their performers. Hearing this makes me sick to my stomach. Bill and I always went to Summerfest. We would take our Harley so we could park in the Harley lot for free. The lot was also just outside the main entrance, so it was very convenient and it made us feel like part of the Harley group (although maybe the wimpy part). We would enjoy walking around eating, and listening to the bands. We skipped the booths where people were enjoying a beer or two or three...

Bill and I would look around at all the food stands, seeing what looked good to each of us. It's very difficult to go down Memory Lane with this—I remember everything, but it hurts. We would have so much fun, walking around hand in hand. And, if we were lucky, our favorite band, REO, would be playing. We loved so many of their songs; our favorite was "I Can't Fight This Feeling." We would sing along with the band, just as everyone else was doing. Bill would often stand behind me, with his arms wrapped around me, both of us swaying with the music.

Wonderful memories are painful to think about...

Friday, June 7, 2013

I met with Ken again today. He's starting to read me better. He knows my tension is high, and he talks about hoping to find a middle ground between being happy and being depressed.

That would be a big jump for me, especially when right now I'm feeling so depressed.

Saturday, June 8, 2013

Today was the big day for Fr. Pat's family to move from Ohio to our town. Quite a few of the church's congregation came to help them move into their house. And thank goodness—they had plenty of stuff!

Monday, June 10, 2013

I had a session with Diana today and let her know just how on edge I am. I'm very nervous about Saturday because I've agreed to go to my nephew David's graduation and his party at my house afterward. Scott and Debbie—and their family—are doing all the work and inviting everyone. I'll know most of the people who are coming, but it'll be a big group, so I'm nervous.

Diana was concerned, saying it was a lot to take on. But I explained that Debbie was bringing all the food, and I just had to make a pumpkin pie, David's favorite. I guess we'll see how I do. Hopefully I won't go into hiding.

Wednesday, June 12, 2013

Today is my session with Dr. John. I told him the same story I told Diana about the graduation and party on Saturday. He agreed this was a lot for me to take on, but he said if it gets too much for me, I should separate myself from the group here and there. And if it really gets to be too much, go to the hospital. Unfortunately, I knew I had to get through it for David's sake.

Friday, June 14, 2013

And of course I told the same story to Ken today. It was a repetitive week in my sessions, but Saturday was a big deal. I needed to know what they thought. And since it was so close to the anniversary of Bill's accident, I was getting shaky.

Saturday, June 15, 2013

Today is David's graduation from high school. It means a lot to me that the family wants me so closely included. I'm very close to my nephew and his sister, Stephanie—I feel more like their grandmother than their aunt. But I was worried about going to this graduation because it would be crowded and noisy. And I knew I would be thinking about Bill not being there, mostly because Bill was David's godfather. But with help from Scott (Bill's brother), Debbie (my sister-in- law), and Stephanie, I got through it. I was able to be with David for his graduation. He'll be heading off to college in the fall, so it's nice to be part of this change in his life.

I headed into the evening party feeling nervous and wondering if I was going to be able to do this. But Scott and Debbie had everything planned out; I didn't have to do anything but talk with the guests (which also was a challenge.). It helped that Bill's female cousins came too, so I sat with them. They were talking plenty, which meant I didn't have to say much.

As the party ended, I was amazed that I had done so well. Debbie and her crew cleaned up, so I didn't have hours of work ahead of me.

Monday, June 17, 2013

Finally the day arrived for Lady's therapy dog test. When I was called into the testing room, I tried to stay calm so Lady wouldn't get too anxious.

The woman who would be administering the test watched Lady move around. She asked about Lady's limp, and I explained she has arthritis in her knee area and that I give her pain pills as needed. She looked concerned, and I explained I would never have Lady walk more than is comfortable for her. She had me walk around with Lady a little, and then she told me that she wasn't going to give Lady the test because she felt that people would get nervous watching Lady limping. I again explained that I wouldn't do more than Lady was comfortable doing. It didn't matter; she had already decided not to test Lady.

I was devastated. I had plans to visit small places like nursing homes with Lady; she would love the attention, and she is such a sweet dog that I knew she would be a pleasure to others. But no go. I wasn't going to be able to get a license for her. I felt angry that they didn't even give Lady a chance. All the lessons we went through, to not even be tested—I was sorely disappointed.

Tuesday, June 18, 2013

I felt very edgy on the anniversary of the evening before the day of Bill's accident. At my appointment with Diana today, I told her about my tension. I was even having trouble listening to her because I was so nervous and saddened by my memories of this horrible event.

When I got home, I started drinking. Not a lot, but I was trying to settle my nerves. I decided to get to bed early so I would sleep through the time of the event the next morning. But my mind was already racing...

Four years ago, Bill and I got home from a nice motorcycle ride and dinner. He was exhausted after working a twelve- hour shift that day, so we decided to watch TV in bed; it was a way we often unwound from the day. Then it started to thunder and rain outside. We were trying to settle down in bed, still watching TV, but the storm continued to increase in volume. We both were aware that a phone call could come, asking Bill to come back to work. It had happened many times before.

We finally turned off the TV and were trying to fall asleep when the phone rang. It was Bill's work, of course, telling him they needed him because the rain was filling up the tunnels, and alarms were going off. I was worried because he was so tired. I turned the TV back on and heard the weather reports saying many streets were flooding. I was scared to think of Bill driving to work, and I repeatedly told him to be careful. I asked him to call me when he got to work. He left, and I drifted off to sleep. And that was the last time I saw Bill before the accident that claimed his life.

Wednesday, June 19, 2013

I was grateful to have an appointment with Dr. John today, because I was so upset about the anniversary of Bill's accident that I was entertaining thoughts of ending my life. All I wanted was to be reunited with Bill. Before and after seeing Dr. John, my day was filled with continued thoughts of what happened four years ago...

Early that morning, I awoke to the phone ringing. I had trouble finding the phone in the dark, so the answering machine kicked in. It was Bill's partner that night, Cal. He was telling me that Bill had been burned and that they were heading to the hospital. I panicked, not knowing how bad he was or what hospital he was going to. But thank goodness Cal tried calling again, and this time I got to the phone. Bill had received steam burns all over this body and was being taken to St. Mary's Hospital. In a panic, I called Beth, who arrived quickly at my home, and we headed to the hospital.

Bill was in an emergency room being treated; we found Cal in the waiting room. He gave me the details of how Bill had gone down into a tunnel to check it out, when the heat surrounded him. He had managed to climb out of the tunnel, but his body was badly burned by the steam.

I got to see Bill shortly before he was transferred to the burn center upstairs. He still looked like Bill, thank goodness. His eyes were closed, but he acknowledged my voice. At least he knew I was there. They took him upstairs, but I had to stay in a waiting room while they were getting him settled. I sat and prayed and prayed and prayed.

These memories flooded my heart, even while I sat and talked with Dr. John. He knew how awful I was feeling. He asked if I thought I should go into the hospital. I knew I probably should, but I just wasn't ready for that; I wanted to go home and end everything.

Dr. John made an appointment to see me again this Friday.

Thursday, June 20, 2013

I sat at home all day, thinking about Bill continuously. I missed him so dearly. Nothing seemed to take away the pain of missing him. I was filled to overflowing with thoughts of the events of four years ago...

When I was finally allowed into Bill's room, his face had started to swell, and he was in pain. They had to wait until his vitals settled down before giving him more pain medications. I talked with him, and he heard my voice. I told him I loved him, and he started moving around, trying to talk, but he couldn't because they had intubated him. He kept struggling, but I finally realized what he was trying to say. I told him I knew he loved me too.

When he heard this, he gave me a strong nod, and then he settled down. That was the last movement I ever saw Bill make, because they gave him a paralyzing drug so he wouldn't hurt himself further.

With all of these thoughts whirling in my head, I decided to get drunk. I made one drink, than another. But my thoughts about Bill were so overwhelming that I forgot about the alcohol. I went to find a razor blade, and then I started experimenting with them on my wrist. The alcohol had given me false courage.

As I watched my blood dripping down the drain, I decided that was enough for tonight. I was exhausted, and I decided to go to bed.

Friday, June 21, 2013

In the morning I saw Rosemary and told her how bad I had been feeling. She was so sweet—she let me talk and talk about how difficult the memories were for me. How hard it was missing Bill so much. She talked about how difficult it was for her also, missing her husband.

Then I showed her my arm and admitted how I had used a razor blade on it the night before. Obviously I hadn't gone far enough to kill myself, but I was edging closer to suicide. Rosemary immediately expressed her concern for me, but I told her I was seeing Dr. John this afternoon. She reminded me to tell him everything, and I agreed. She also asked me to call her if I needed help—or just another voice to listen to.

Later today, in my session with Dr. John, I explained what I had done with my wrist, and he took a look at it. He repeated that he wanted me to go back into the hospital, but I objected; I just didn't want to. He said if I was in trouble, I should come in immediately, or call 911.

I asked if he would be my doctor if I went into the hospital again. He said he hadn't returned to inpatient work yet; that would happen in a few weeks. I told him I didn't want to go in unless he was my doctor, so I would wait.

Back at home, my thoughts drifted again, to four years ago. My long vigil at the hospital's burn unit was just beginning. Bill was in intensive care and looked like he was asleep, but they told me he could hear me talking. So that's what I did—I talked and talked. About his condition and how it had happened, about how much I loved him (and knew he loved me), and about every happy story I could think of that involved the two of us.

These memories of talking to Bill as he lay helpless in the burn unit made me feel like I was drowning in depression. I felt a strong surge of panic. I checked my phone messages and found one from Rosemary. I called her and told her a little of what was going on. I felt so bad then, because she was instantly worried. I hated doing that to her. But I also told her that I had just seen Dr. John, who warned me that I should return to the hospital if I felt tempted to hurt myself. I repeated to her I wouldn't do anything and that I was feeling quite tired, so I would go to bed. I hung up, crawled into bed, and fell asleep immediately.

Saturday, June 22, 2013

Today I saw Beth. She knew what time of year it was, so she suggested we go rummaging to get my mind off things. That helped me quite a bit, because I got interested in looking at all the items in the thrift stores and yard sales. I also got a kick out of the fact that I was the only one who bought anything. Beth's side of the car was empty, and she let me know it.

Exhausted from shopping, we agreed it was time for a lunch break. We went to a Mexican restaurant to eat and, of course, have a margarita. I was comfortable eating Mexican food because it was something Bill didn't like, so he and I were never in a Mexican restaurant. After we finished lunch, Beth dropped me off at home. I called Rosemary to reassure her I was okay.

Sunday, June 23, 2013

Terry called to tell me that Roger's implanted defibrillator had gone off twice, and he was in the hospital. I was so scared—I had been worried about myself, but here was a larger fear. *Please don't let Roger die,* I pleaded with God. I couldn't take that.

I went to the hospital to visit Roger, and he looked okay, but he was worried. He described the shocks from the defibrillator as feeling as if he were hit by lightning. They knocked him down to his knees and made him afraid to move, in case the defibrillator went off again.

It was difficult for me to visit Roger in the hospital, especially during the same time of year that Bill had been in the hospital. I was looking at the machines and thinking they were similar to the machines that had been connected to Bill. I kept my thoughts to myself, though; Roger didn't need to worry about me right now.

The hospital was running numerous tests on him, for which I was grateful. He had many heart problems, and he never felt very good. And they found a problem: he hadn't been taking one of his medications. Roger explained that he had run out of that medication and was waiting for his appointment with Dr. Steven. That was a big mistake because that medication helped keep his heart thumping in the correct rhythm. So now, without the medication, his heart had gone into an incorrect rhythm. That arrhythmia probably would have killed him if not for the defibrillator. He stayed one more day in the hospital, and then they released him.

This event caused me to temporarily stop thinking about my sorrow. But now that Roger was getting better, I was back to thinking about myself and Bill.

Wednesday, June 26, 2013

I was at my appointment with Dr. John, telling him how I had been edgy all weekend and into this week, worrying about Roger and immersed in my grief over Bill. I explained what was going on medically with my brother, but that he was doing better and was home again.

I told him my mind was on suicide, and I was drinking some. I just kept on thinking back to four years ago, when I had been visiting Bill every day in the hospital. I wanted so desperately to be with him now.

Dr. John again suggested again that I should be in the hospital. I was starting to agree with him, but I wanted to go home first. If I entered the hospital, I would need Roger and Terry to take Lady. And I wasn't sure if Roger was doing well enough to handle another dog in his house right now. My thoughts ran in circles. *Should I go into the hospital, or not?* I wondered.

Thursday, June 27, 2013

We had Bible study in the evening. I was having trouble concentrating and talking with the others. I kept thinking that I should probably go into the hospital again.

I knew Fr. Patrick was watching me and was concerned about me. He told me later that he knew I was having trouble concentrating and that he was very worried.

Saturday, June 29, 2013

I woke up to a phone call from Gary, letting me know Beth's mother was in the hospital. Sadly, she was terminal. Her vitals had decreased quite a lot, and she didn't want any additional resuscitation. The family was waiting with her until the end. I felt quite saddened because I had known Eva for most of my life. Just like my mother was Beth's second mom, Eva was my second mom.

When I was a teenager, Eva had invited me to many of their family outings, such as swimming at Moose Lake, which was about half an hour from Milwaukee. It had a great beach area, and we would swim for hours. Sometimes Beth's dad would get in the water and we would have chicken fights. And Beth's mom would always bring a basket full of food. Her breaded chicken was wonderful.

Beth's family also would go to Schwaubenhof, a German dance hall near us. Eva made German-style dresses for Beth and me, called Dirndls. It was such fun dancing polkas and other dances in those dresses.

I sat by my phone, thinking about how difficult this was on their family, watching and waiting for Eva to die. I remembered how Roger and I had waited by my mom's bedside, watching as she died. It was horrible. My heart was saddened, thinking about them. But I was also thinking about my own situation. Just as I was deciding whether I should be readmitted, Beth's family was going through their own crisis. I couldn't go into the hospital now.

Later in the day, Gary called me again to let me know that Eva had passed. I asked if I could see Beth or do anything, but Gary said not now. Beth didn't really want to talk at the moment. I decided to wait to see when the funeral would be. Beth and Gary's grown daughters had arrived in town in time to see their grandma, and they were staying at Beth's house. I knew that would help Beth immensely.

Sunday, June 30, 2013

Terry called this morning and woke me up. Roger was having chest pains and had gone to the hospital. I let her know I would be there as quickly as possible.

I couldn't believe it. Serious news, two days in a row. I thanked God that I hadn't gone into the hospital. I had to be here for both families.

I called Beth; she said they're going to make the funeral arrangements tomorrow. She was trying to hold in her emotions, and I guess I know what that's like. I told her she's in my prayers. I guess there's nothing else for me to do right now.

Six years ago on this date, my mom died after suffering with Alzheimer's for quite a few years. She lived with Bill and me, so we were able to care for her, but in 2007 she was quickly worsening.

It was so difficult for all of us during that time. My mom had stopped recognizing Bill over the past year, and that was difficult because she had loved Bill. But now she was afraid of this big guy she didn't know anymore. And worse yet, she was starting to forget who I was. She would walk up to me with such anger in her eyes, and tell me that I wasn't her daughter. I always found that odd, because it wasn't like I was telling her I was her daughter; she was bringing it up on her own. She must have been so confused. It was frightening and horribly sad.

I saw my therapist, Diana, this afternoon. She also was concerned about my state of mind. I let her know about my thoughts of suicide. I told her I should probably go into the hospital, but there was too much going on in my life right now.

Roger has been released from the hospital, but we are all still worried about him. His case is so complicated, it seems that too many things could go wrong.

Tuesday, July 2, 2013

I met with Ken again. This time I explained how fragile I am and that I want to end it all. Like everyone else, he said that I should go into the hospital, but I told him I just have too much to think about at the moment. My brother's health is still in jeopardy, so I'm concerned about adding Lady to his household right now. And Eva's funeral is tomorrow; I have to be there. I'm also concerned that Dr. John isn't seeing inpatients yet. I don't want to have another doctor.

Ken said he would talk with Dr. John and see what could be done. He called me later today to tell me what Dr. John said: If I was hospitalized, Dr. John would talk with the covering doctor, and they weren't to change my medications without his consent. That had me feeling much better. I was to see Dr. John on Friday, and we would talk then.

Wednesday, July 3, 2013

Today was Eva's funeral. Julie, my step-daughter, had called me to say she would be at the funeral. She knows Beth well, so it was nice for her to be able to attend. She would be coming from work.

At Eva's service, I looked at all the pictures and marveled at the flood of memories they brought back. Happy memories on a sad occasion. It was hard to believe so much time has passed since those days on the beach.

After the funeral we met at a restaurant for lunch. This was especially difficult for me, because Bill and I had come to this restaurant many times. My stomach was in a knot, so I ordered a Southern Comfort and Coke. I couldn't believe it when it arrived. It was in a tall glass—like a double drink. And it was strong. I decided that was good; it got me through the meal.

When I finally got home, I checked my messages. There was a message from Terry saying that Roger had suffered multiple shocks from his defibrillator and was back in the hospital. I fed Lady, quickly took her outside to do her business, and then rushed to the hospital. I was scared to death.

When I got to Roger's room, he looked frightened, but he was glad to be in the hospital. He wasn't in pain, but he was experiencing some kind of strange sensations in his chest, and that was worrying him. He also felt dizzy. He said if he was home he would be in a panic. Then he and Terry explained what had just happened.

Roger received the first shock in his basement. He had to try to get upstairs to get Terry. As he struggled on the steps, his defibrillator sent out another shock. He continued to struggle up the stairs into the living room where Terry was, but he received two more shocks before they got to their car.

They decided to drive to the hospital because the hospital was close, and waiting for an ambulance could mean more shocks. They got about a mile from their house when a police cruiser pulled them over. Terry got out of the car, and the officer said he stopped her because a light was out on the lower part of the car window—an extra brake light. That was crazy because it's just an extra light, not a required light.

Terry yelled to the officer that her husband was having a heart attack, and she got back in the car. She had barely moved the car ahead when additional squad cars pulled in front of her. She again got out of the car, and the officer told her he had called for an ambulance.

Roger, hearing this, got out of the car to try to explain the urgency of the situation. But as he stood up, he received another shock, knocking him to the sidewalk. And they kept coming. Roger urgently prayed as shock after shock continued. He felt he was going to die, so he yelled to Terry that he loved her.

The ambulance finally arrived, and amazingly they got him to the hospital without another shock. Once in cardiac intensive care, they were able to give him an IV that calmed his heart rhythm. In all, he had eleven shocks.

I was very upset, thinking about Roger, thinking about the funeral I had just attended, and nearly obsessed with thoughts about Bill. Here I was in a hospital room, worrying about Roger and watching the monitors. Again, too many reminders of Bill in the hospital. But it was my brother—I couldn't be any other place.

As serious as this was, at least they had him stabilized. He was scared, but glad to be in the hospital. I felt like the whole world was crashing around me. I kept pretty quiet at the hospital, anxious to go home after a long, hard, day.

Thursday, July 4, 2013

Early in the morning, Roger had a catheterization done to better determine what was happening with his heart. He learned that he could probably have his choice of having multiple stents or bypass surgery. But there was another problem: They found a muscle over his heart, which was probably formed from a heart attack. Roger had a heart attack at age forty, but this showed he may have had another. This muscle, and the blockage of some arteries, was probably causing his erratic heart rhythm.

Normally, since I had lost Bill, I would stay at home on the Fourth of July. I could no longer stand the sight of anything that reminded me of the holiday, because I had such happy memories of being with Bill. When the kids were young, we would have a large picnic in our back yard, inviting some of our friends. Most often that would include Beth's family, Scott's family, and a few times, Dave's family. We would have games for the kids, and all kinds of food, of course, including food off the grill.

As the kids grew older and had their own plans, Bill and I would take one of the motorcycles and drive around until we found a Fourth of July festivity. Sometimes there would be a band, but what we really liked was the food.

But here I was on Independence Day, sitting in a hospital room, this time visiting Roger. He looked more relaxed today. We were still waiting for the heart surgeon to see if he could have an open heart bypass. And Roger really wanted to know if they could repair the muscle on his heart at the same time. But no doctors were doing rounds today. We would have to wait until tomorrow.

I got home very tired and ready to go to bed. But first I wanted to call both Fr. Pat and Fr. Russ, our long-time friend, to tell them about Roger. Both said they would visit him. I liked that—I knew he needed as many blessings as possible. I played with Lady, who had been alone most of the day. Finally, I watched some TV and went to bed.

Friday, July 5, 2013

I visited with Roger at the hospital until I had to leave to see Dr. John. Before I got there, Roger had seen the heart surgeon. They knew Roger wanted to have the bypass and hopefully have the muscle removal at the same time. But he still hadn't been told when the surgery would be. It might be Saturday or Monday. Roger was looking better. He was even sitting in a chair today.

At my appointment with Dr. John, I sat down and told him about all the recent crises in my life. He was very concerned about how they were affecting me. He told me he wants to hear all about when the surgery is going to be. And he was very aware that tomorrow is the anniversary of Bill's death. He told me once again that if it became too much for me to handle, I should go into the hospital.

I called Roger to see if he had any more information. Yes he did—he was going to have to wait until Tuesday to have a test regarding the muscle on his heart. So nothing could be done until after the weekend. Roger sounded sad, and I felt sad as I reminded him of tomorrow's anniversary. He already knew. I told him I wouldn't be visiting tomorrow, but if anything came up with him, to call me.

Saturday, July 6, 2013

Today is the anniversary of Bill's death. Once again, I found it very important to be alone today with my thoughts of Bill. And, hopefully, to be alone with Bill—to feel his presence.

Most of the people who know me are used to my wanting to be alone on the anniversary, so I knew the day would be quiet.

I wanted to start the day by going to the cemetery, but I felt frightened. I'm not sure why; since Bill died, every Sunday after church I would go visit his grave. It was very difficult, and a time of many tears, but I wanted to go. I felt I should go. But lately, something has happened and I don't know why, but I've had a sense of dread before entering the cemetery. One day I drove all the way and couldn't get myself to drive inside. It's been bothering me quite a lot, especially since I don't understand the change.

After taking my morning pills, I felt a little calmer, so I decided to make the trip right away. On the way there I was getting increasingly nervous. I entered the cemetery and followed the road, knowing exactly where to stop. I pulled up to the spot and parked. I could see Bill's headstone from the car. I sat and sat. I talked with Bill; I talked with God; but I was unable to get out of the car. I decided I would wait until another time. I drove home in tears, feeling so sad.

Back in the house, I still felt bad that I hadn't gotten out of the car. *Maybe this is something to mention to Dr. John or Ken?* I thought. I played with Lady some, and then decided to try to find something on TV to calm myself. Not feeling right about anything, I turned the TV off and sat in my chair, staring into space. It was so quiet. I felt the keen, knife-like pain of loneliness. I missed Bill so much.

Sunday, July 7, 2013

I couldn't face going to church. I wanted to be close to God, but I wasn't ready to see all the other people. There were just too many things going wrong. I sat in the house thinking about Bill, and thinking about Roger in the hospital. I wanted to go into the psych hospital myself, but I couldn't now. It was difficult to hide just how awful I was feeling from everyone.

This is going to be another rough week.

Monday, July 8, 2013

When I went to visit Roger at the hospital, I found him curled up in his bed. He told me he didn't want to talk, but that I could talk to him. He was in some kind of emotional pain, but I didn't know why. I tried to ask, but he said he didn't want to talk. So I just sat with him for a while. Finally, he told me they couldn't do the heart surgery because his heart was too fragile. They were going to do two or three stents tomorrow instead. After that he said it was probably best that I leave.

I knew he was too upset to talk anymore, so I said goodbye and told him I would return tomorrow.

We had all hoped that he was going to have the heart surgery. I guess we thought that would fix everything. It was hard to hear that his heart is too fragile, and that makes me nervous about the surgery to insert the stents. *Is this going to be dangerous for Roger?* I worried.

Tuesday, July 9, 2013

Robin, Fr. Pat's wife, called me to see how I was doing. I told her I'm very worried about Roger having the stent procedure today. It's a very serious procedure for him, because of all the complications. Robin told me she would pick me up and go with me to the hospital to sit with Terry in the waiting room. That sounded good to me, so I agreed.

At the hospital, the three of us waited for a while, until the cardiologist came out to see us. He told us the procedure was successful, and Roger was in recovery. Thank God! We were all so relieved.

Wednesday, July 10, 2013

I went to my appointment with Dr. John and told him I was thrilled that Roger had come through the procedure so well. I had many different emotions running back and forth in my mind. I was thinking about Bill, then Roger, and then back again to Bill. With all these emotions, I was a wreck. I still felt like going into the hospital, but I had to deal with these other things first. Dr. John told me that when I was ready to enter the hospital, he now had his privileges back. I was thrilled.

I went to visit Roger. He looked tired, but he looked better than he had on Tuesday. Some of the worry was off his face, but he was still nervous about his defibrillator. We asked if having the stents put in would help with keeping his defibrillator from shocking him again. We didn't really get the answers, but my mind was thinking the answer was no.

Thursday, July 11, 2013

I called to say hi to Roger. He was very tired, so he said I didn't need to come to the hospital. Terry was going to be there after work. That was probably good, because I was still so tired from all the stress.

Friday, July 12, 2013

Roger was released today. I found out when I talked with him on the phone. I didn't need to go to the hospital because Terry was picking him up after work. I figured he would be quite tired once he got home, so I didn't need to visit.

Again, I was an emotional wreck, but I held it in because I didn't know when I might be getting some help.

Saturday, July 13, 2013

I had emailed Beth a couple of days ago about getting together today, but she wasn't ready to do anything yet. I could understand that. I decided it was a good day to take it easy.

Sunday, July 14, 2013

I went to church. I tried to keep quiet and calm during the service, but I was close to crying many times. I was wearing all my emotions on my sleeve. Since the crises had died down for now, I decided it was time to go into the hospital again.

It amazed me how I knew when I had to hold it together for others, but then the day would come when I knew I had to be readmitted. And that day was today.

After the mass I decided to tell the people who attend the Bible study at my house that I wouldn't be there. They could still use my house; I just wouldn't be there. And, of course, I told Fr. Pat and Robin. I was fighting the tears in my eyes, but I needed to ask if they could take care of Lady while I was gone. Roger wasn't ready to have another dog in his house yet.

Robin told me their dog didn't do well with other dogs, but she thought Megan would like to stay at my house and take care of her there. She just needed to talk to Megan first, of course. Luckily, Megan was in full agreement, and I was thrilled because I didn't know who else to ask.

Megan came over to my house after church so I could show her the house and where Lady's food was. It didn't take long to show her, so with that taken care of, I started to pack for the hospital.

Another trip to the input area. It was crowded. There would be a long wait. Back to all the paperwork—including telling them to admit me under Dr. John. And now the wait. I had arrived at the input area at 7:30 p.m. It was now getting close to 9:00 p.m.

Once all the paperwork was completed, I walked down the hall toward the original unit I had been in. I was glad for that—I liked the set-up there, more than the other unit. Back to the orientation time in my room with the nurses' aides; it seemed to go fast. It had been a long day, and I was tired and hungry, but the nurses didn't offer me anything to eat this time. I guess that was okay. After my medications, I was going right to sleep.

Once in bed, I felt like I could just lie here forever. I knew I'd be seeing Dr. John in the morning, and that was good. I was emotionally tired—between worrying about Roger and Beth, I felt exhausted. Not physically, but mentally. As I drifted off to sleep, I thought about Bill.

Monday, July 15, 2013

I awoke to daylight, wanting to know what time it was. It drove me nuts that there wasn't a clock in the room. Since I had no idea what time it was, I tried to fall asleep again. I lay there, thinking about Bill and everything that had been happening the last couple of weeks. And I thought about Lady, knowing I already missed her so much. I wasn't afraid of sleeping too long, though, because I knew the call for breakfast would wake me up anyway.

And that it did. Time to get up. I splashed some water on my face, combed my hair, and headed to the nurses' area where our trays were. I didn't know what I was getting. The first day was always ordered for you. I sat down at a vacant table and lifted the cover. Yay! French toast and sausage that smelled and looked delicious. I was hungry.

After breakfast, I went back to my room to be alone. I wanted to isolate in the hospital as much as at home. But then Dr. John entered my room. He was always welcome, and we talked for a while. I explained that I was still very tense after these last couple of weeks. He said that was to be expected, and I should just try to relax before the sessions started.

The rest of the morning was filled with sessions with the regular medical doctor, therapist, case worker, and so on. And then I was cleared to go to the afternoon sessions.

Tuesday, July 16, 2013

I called Roger. He found out he had to go back to the hospital. It had been five days since the surgery, and he still felt horrible. I was worried.

Wednesday, July 17, 2013

Roger only stayed a day and was discharged. He was becoming more tense every day, worrying his defibrillator could go off at any time. He felt safer in the hospital, but they said he was okay to stay home.

Thursday, July 18, 2013

I called Roger and learned that he's in the hospital again. He and Terry had a horrible evening. It was so scary. He 's having difficulty almost every day.

Friday, July 19, 2013

I called Beth, and she was upset that I had finally called her to let her know I was in the psych hospital again. I was trying to explain all the problems that Roger was still having, but I don't know if she heard me, because she was furious about the next topic. She had to do all the work for Becky's bridal shower because I was in the hospital, and I probably wouldn't even make it to the shower. I told her I'd be getting out before that, and I would do anything she needed. She told me, no, she and Katie (her daughter) had most everything done.

I felt horrible that Beth thought I didn't care about the shower, but I was dealing with two things—being in the psych hospital and worrying about Roger. I started to tell her that I'd help as soon as I got out, but she began to calm down and told me to just get better, and she'd see me at the shower. It was being held on Beth's birthday, July 27. That date worked beautifully, because both daughters would be coming home that weekend anyway to celebrate Beth's birthday. They just had to have a shower first.

Saturday, July 20, 2013

I was worried about Roger, and the shower, but I was also worried about whether I was getting anywhere in the hospital. My mind was on everything stressful. I was thinking about asking Dr. John to discharge me. It would be a long weekend for thought.

Sunday, July 21, 2013

Roger called me; he's being discharged from the hospital today. And he sounds more scared than I've ever heard him. He was telling me that I would have to be at his house tomorrow morning when Terry went to work. He couldn't be alone because he was so scared that the defibrillator would go off again and he would need to go to the hospital. I told him I would do what I could, but I reminded him that I was in the psych hospital. I would need to talk with Dr. John about being discharged, so I wouldn't be able to get to his house by Monday morning. He kept saying I had to be there.

It was so unlike Roger—I've never heard him like this before. I'm scared and worried about him.

Monday, July 22, 2013

Dr. John came in to see me. After we talked for a bit, he told me he would discharge me today. He said it was a little earlier than he wanted to, but I was calmer than before the hospitalization, and he thought I would do okay since I would be busy with Roger.

He was right; I was worried about Roger. I knew I was going to have to spend a lot of time at his house, but I was also going to need to go to my appointments. I wasn't sure how I was going to be able to accomplish this, but as usual, I was going to try to take it one step at a time, and hopefully, not get too tense.

I called Roger when I got home. He sounded anxious, so I headed to his house and found him in rough shape. Lying on the couch, he was trying to sleep while trying not to move. Bee Gee (one of their cats) seemed worried about what was wrong with Roger. He sat on the couch right in front of Roger's nose, watching him. Bee Gee was possibly just standing guard for his friend.

I told Roger I'd be right over on Tuesday morning, but he said I could wait until noon, when he would be waking up. If anything else happened, he would call me. That would work out great because I would be able to get to my appointment.

Tuesday, July 23, 2013

Another partial day at Roger's house. Today he was feeling slightly more like himself. He said I could leave by 3:00 in the afternoon because Terry would be home in a couple of hours.

Once home, I emailed Beth's daughter, Katie, and asked if there was anything I could do for the shower. She said everything was done, so just relax and come to the shower. I felt guilty that I hadn't helped more.

Wednesday, July 24, 2013

I didn't really feel like I was doing much at Roger's, except for watching TV. I felt it was best if I wasn't moving around, stirring the animals up—especially Roger's two yellow labs. They love getting attention from everyone. So I stayed quiet, and Roger also seemed more relaxed when nothing was happening around him. Luckily I was able to leave for my appointment with Dr. John on time.

Dr. John asked me how I was doing. I told him it was very stressful for me to be worrying about Roger and trying to juggle my schedule around him. I also wished these emergencies hadn't come up so I could have just stayed in the hospital.

Thursday, July 25, 2013

I stopped by Roger's house again today. He is slowly becoming himself again. I know he's still afraid, but I think he's had too many days of just lying on the couch, and he's getting antsy. When I got there, he was carefully doing small jobs around the house, which was good to see. He said that I don't need to come over tomorrow unless I call him. That's good news—I can keep my appointment with Ken.

While I was home in the early evening, Bob (my step-daughter's husband) called. Their baby boy was born today—my grandson! Scott, Bill's brother, picked me up and we headed to the hospital. Entering their room, we saw the little newborn, lying on his mom's legs and looking quite content. Watching him lasted about two minutes, and then I wanted to hold him. I picked him up and sat down in a chair. How precious—holding someone newly born. It was amazing. Holding him was like holding Bill. I knew a piece of Bill was inside this little boy.

Julie announced they had picked a name: William, after her father and brother. But instead of nicknaming him Bill, they decided to call him Will. I'm glad for that—he has his own identity. I love it.

Friday, July 26, 2013

I called Beth to make sure there wasn't something I could do. I told her I would be over on Friday to help out with anything she needed. She said that wasn't necessary, but they wanted to borrow my card tables and chairs. That was no problem.

Saturday, July 27, 2013

Becky's bridal shower. It was a beautiful day, and Katie and her friends had set up the shower in the back yard. It looked elegant. Today was also Beth's birthday, but she wasn't going to get much attention; it would all fall on Becky. It was hard to believe little Becky was now engaged Rebecca. Where did the time go?

We enjoyed the luncheon and watching Becky open her presents while another first was happening: Julie called and let us know she and baby Will were being discharged from the hospital. Bob was picking them up to head to their new home. We all told them to stop by the shower before heading home, but that didn't fly—although we were just kidding.

Sunday, July 28, 2013

After church, I came home to relax in "our" lounge chair. Bill used to often sit in this chair; now it's my favorite place to relax. These last two weeks were filled with so much stress. Now that things are settling down, my thoughts have returned to Bill, and I've been feeling terribly sad and depressed.

August 2013

August was a month of relaxation for me. So much happened before this month that I feel the energy is just drained from me. I go outside to think about gardening, but I just don't have it in me. I flip stations on my TV; nothing seems interesting. Beth has had a busy month, so I haven't seen her much. Roger asks me to come over, but I only visit him occasionally. I go to church on Sundays, but Bible study is cancelled in August. The widows' group has also cancelled their meeting in August. I still go to my three visits a week with Diana, Dr. John, and Ken. Otherwise, I spend a lot of time thinking of Bill and napping in my lounge chair.

Wednesday, September 4, 2013

In my appointment with Dr. John, I let him know I'm still quite anxious. I've been caught up in thinking about Bill and getting to him, which again meant thoughts of suicide. I cried to Dr. John that I couldn't do this anymore. He grew concerned and asked if I had any plans for the weekend. I told him, no, I just wanted to stay home alone. He asked if I would call him over the weekend, so he would know if I was okay. I agreed.

Saturday, September 7, 2013—Labor Day Weekend

I stayed home all day, alone, feeling quite upset and tense. I had a couple of drinks and felt very tired. I stayed up late, knowing I won't be going to church tomorrow. I just don't feel like facing people right now.

Sunday, September 8, 2013—Labor Day Weekend

I mostly sat staring off into space today. By late afternoon I realized I should call Dr. John. He answered my call and asked know how I was doing. I told him I was the same— quite shaky. He asked me to call him the next day to check in again. I knew I was causing him to worry about me, and I felt bad to be bothering him.

Monday, September 9, 2013—Labor Day

David and Sharon (from church) told me they would go car shopping with me today. They had checked, and it was a big sale day for car dealerships. All of them would be open on the holiday—unfortunately for their employees.

Last week I went window shopping for cars online. I was able to see photos of many different cars, so I could tell which ones I liked. Once I eliminated the ones that were too expensive, I decided I liked the Honda Accord the best, so that dealership was first on my list. But before David and Sharon arrived, I called Dr. John. I told him I was still shaky, but I would have company today, and I told him about the car shopping. He said he was glad I was going to be with someone, and he'd see me on Wednesday.

It was funny pulling up to the Honda dealership. There must have been ten dealers all standing outside, ready to help any customer who pulled into the lot. I explained to her what I wanted. They had the car, but they didn't have it in a color I liked. I took it for a test drive and I loved it. I knew if I couldn't get the color I wanted I would probably get it anyway, but I didn't tell her. We put a hold on the car and told them we were going to check with some other dealers.

We tried one more dealer, but they didn't have the right color either. So we went back to the original dealer and lo and behold, they had found the color I wanted at one of their other dealerships. That was a great surprise. I loved the car and bought it.

Wednesday, September 11, 2013

I told Dr. John at my appointment today that I'm still thinking of suicide. Dr. John stated that I've been in this state of mind since the Labor Day weekend. I could tell he was concerned. He started asking me more about how these thoughts affect me. Did I feel a sense of relief that I might get to Bill sooner?

I told him it actually frustrates me, because I haven't gone through with it yet. I started crying, explaining once again that I miss Bill so much I can't stand it. He ended the session without saying much more. He seemed to be in deep thought, maybe trying to figure out how to help me.

I got home and had a wonderful surprise: Julie was at my house with my three-week old grandson, William. I couldn't wait to hold him. As I picked him up and snuggled him, I felt so close to him. So much love. Holding him was giving me joy—followed by sadness—as I pictured Bill holding him, also feeling such love for his grandson. Thank goodness I didn't start crying.

The moment did have its funny part. What I didn't know was that he had just had a good-sized bowel movement. He was laughing and wiggling all over the place. I think he was quite proud of himself while his mom cleaned it all up.

Thursday, September 12, 2013

Dave and Tom are working on repairing the front part of Roger's house. I had a therapy appointment with Ken, and I really didn't need to go to Roger's house today. I'd been feeling quite tense since I got up this morning. By the time I got to Ken's office, I was already feeling shaky. I explained this to him, and then I started crying. I told him I still keep thinking of suicide often. I haven't attempted to do anything, but it's just hanging in my thoughts.

We discussed trying to find a diversion for me—not an easy solution. I've tried many diversions, some good and some not so good. But my mind never stops thinking of Bill for long. And when I think of Bill, I think of how I want to be with him.

As we talked, I quieted down some, and soon our time was up. I left still feeling shaky.

This evening we had our Thursday night Bible study. Near the end, the discussion focused on death and God's will. I was fighting back my tears, but I could feel them welling up in me. I tried to quickly get up from my chair and leave the room, as quietly as possible, but my quick movements probably alarmed everyone. I sat in a living room chair, and there it came—and not just tears this time.

I was sobbing as Sharon came into the living room and put her arms around me. She told me she was also grieving the sudden death of her cousin, who had been around her age. He had died in a motorcycle accident. She acknowledged that her loss wasn't on the level of losing my husband, but I told her I realized that she was mourning the death of someone close to her, and that it still hurts.

Robin, the pastor's wife, came in the living room next and also gave me a hug. All of those in the Bible study knew of my long-lasting grief, so they weren't too surprised when I would start to cry. Fr. Pat came into the room and asked if I would forgive him for not watching the conversation more closely; I quickly said that it wasn't his fault at all. Unfortunately I was still crying, so I don't know how convincing I was. Fr. Pat and Robin decided to leave me with Sharon, and all of the others also followed them out of the house.

Sharon stayed a while longer while I was still crying. Finally, I slowed down and told her it was okay. She asked if I had taken my pills, and I said that was a good idea. She made sure I took them before she left. By then I felt so tired, I just straightened things up a bit, took Lady outside briefly, and then headed for the bedroom. I quickly said my prayers because I was so tired that I knew I was going to fall asleep soon. And sleep I did.

Friday, September 13, 2013

I awoke feeling horrible. I again felt shaky like yesterday, and that surprised me because I usually feel calmer in the morning. But I also felt exhausted. I figured crying so hard the night before had worn out my body.

I sat in the living room expecting to fall asleep in the chair, but I was shaky and couldn't sleep. It was very uncomfortable being too tired to do anything, but too shaky to let myself sleep. Outside it was a beautiful day—not too hot, so I knew it was ideal to get some yard work done. I wasn't going to visit Roger today, so that was a second reason to get outside.

I finally talked myself into getting dressed and going outside. I still felt exhausted, but I thought I'd try to work for a while and then take a break. I think I lasted fifteen minutes before I decided to come back inside. I sat for a while, still feeling the same, so I headed back outside for maybe a half hour this time. I spent my day in this strange back-and-forth routine.

I also received a couple calls from members of the Bible study, checking to see if I was okay. They were all worried that they had said something wrong. I felt bad that I had upset everyone, and tried to explain that it was me. The topic had simply made me think of Bill, and my emotions had built from there.

As the day went on, I mostly rested, feeling lousy. I knew I had a busy day tomorrow. First, I had a widows' group luncheon, which I was looking forward to going to. I hadn't been there for about three months, and I wanted to get back into attending the monthly meetings. Then, later in the day, our church was going to celebrate our church feast day— another way of saying we were all bringing food for a food fest. Truthfully, we had a bishop coming into town and he was also giving us a talk. He would celebrate with us the next day.

Saturday, September 14, 2013

When I awoke this morning, I felt exhausted and jittery as usual. I didn't understand why I was still feeling this bad. But I wanted to go to the widows' group luncheon, so I started my morning routine of feeding Lady, taking her out, sitting a while until she was finished, and then taking my pills. I managed to get showered and dressed, going through that routine slowly until I saw it was time to leave.

I walked into the room where the widows' group was meeting. Their chatter hit me right away, and I started to tear up. I walked around a bit until I saw Rosemary. She was talking with someone, so I went to the registration table to get a name tag. Rosemary saw me and came to say she was delighted that I came. I teared up more, just wanting to sit down. Rosemary had me sit next to her, which was great.

Before lunch, there was a speaker who talked about gratitude and thankfulness. She was a good speaker, but I continued to question my trouble with being thankful for much of anything anymore. I knew I should be, since God had given me so much, but with so many of my loved ones gone, that perspective was troublesome to me.

Lunch was delicious, and the conversation at the table was good. I was a bit more relaxed, and glad I had come.

Chris, one of the four initial members that formed the group, sat down next to me. I had meant to speak with her because Rosemary had let me know they had talked about me.

Rosemary was so sweet. She was often worried about me, with good reason, and would call to check on me, and she would pray for me. The group has a prayer list, and she kept me on it.

Chris and I started talking, and for some reason, I told her about my book being published. She wanted to know the details. After I had explained what my book was about, Chris said it would be nice to have a book of personal accounts from the widows. I liked the idea immediately, agreeing that to have short stories or just a meaningful paragraph about each widow would be a wonderful book for other widows to share. I suggested she explain the idea to the widows and set up times for me to interview each one. I could take notes and decide on what to write about later.

We were both excited about the idea for a new book. While she went to talk with someone else, Rosemary came back to talk with me. I told her about our idea, and she was elated. She said, "See, I knew there was a reason God wanted you to be here. He is leading you in the direction He wants you to go.

I thought a lot about that on the way home.

I had a few hours to rest before the church function tonight. I sat in my usual living room chair, hoping to fall asleep, but again I was too tense to relax. So I let my thoughts go where they always go—with Bill.

And then—thank goodness—I remembered I had to bring brownies to the church celebration. I didn't have the energy or desire to make them, but I knew I had to do it. I got up and felt disgusted with myself for complaining about such a simple dessert. I whipped up a box of brownie mix and added chocolate chips to make the brownies especially yummy—and full of calories.

I've been good about watching my diet the last couple of weeks. My godchild Becky's wedding is only two weeks away, and the dress I want to wear is awfully tight. Having two big meals today with a choice of desserts isn't exactly the diet I've been trying to do. I told myself I would need to watch what I ate tonight, but that was a joke. I knew all those homemade things would be too good to ignore.

And I was right. I had a plateful of delicious food and desserts, and a few leftover brownies to take home. Okay… start the diet again on Monday. And maybe get some exercise in there too!

Sunday, September 15, 2013

I sure didn't feel like getting up this morning, but I told too many people yesterday that I would see them today in church. Afterward, as I left church to go to my car, it started raining. I was glad because my yard needed to be watered, but I had wanted to garden today. I sat down in the house and started my thinking, yet again.

Sunday, September 22, 2013

Roger called me this afternoon. He's been admitted to the hospital again. His blood pressure spiked to 180 over 120; then, at the hospital, it went down to 80 over 60. More tests to be taken. I'm worried about him, but he said not to bother coming. Terry would be arriving soon, and he was probably going to be discharged.

Monday, September 23, 2013

I feel worried about so many things, and those worries are causing me to desperately want to be with Bill. I'm lost in my thoughts most of the day. My depression weighs heavily on me. I decided I should try suicide again, but changed my mind because of what Roger was going through. It didn't seem fair to put him through anything else since he was having his own emergency.

Tuesday, September 24, 2013

I spent the morning sitting in a living room chair, again lost in my thoughts. The phone rang; it was Rosemary, from my widows' group. It had been a while since we talked, and she wanted to see how I was doing. She quickly picked up on my mood and wanted to know what was going on. I explained what I was thinking about, and she instantly began to worry. She asked if I was available to meet for supper, and we decided to meet later at a restaurant.

I tried to spend the afternoon gardening. I still needed to pull weeds before I could put down a layer of newspaper and then mulch on top. I wanted it to be a while before I would have to weed the same areas again. But even as I worked, the same thoughts stayed with me all day. At times it felt like a heavy burden just to move around.

This evening, when I arrived at the restaurant, I saw Rosemary. She was already seated at a table. We hugged, and Rosemary noted that I wasn't even able to pull off a small smile. "No, not today," I told her. We got in line for a sandwich and beverage, and sat at the table Rosemary had saved for us.

She wanted to know what was going on, but I was struggling with the words. I finally let her know that my desire for death had led me to cutting my wrist with the razor blade, but I got scared to cut deep enough to do any real harm. And I let her know I was also thinking about taking all my pills. As I struggled to eat, Rosemary told me how worried she was about me. She let me know that when we held hands in prayer, she felt my hands shaking. I told her I was seeing Dr. John tomorrow, but she was nervous about tonight. She didn't know if I was going to be safe.

She decided that we should talk with Fr. Patrick. I didn't really want to do that, but she insisted, saying we would make the call together. We went out to my car, and I dialed his number on my cell phone. He answered; I told him I was having trouble. I could tell that he was picking up on my mood quickly. I explained I was here with Rosemary, and that she wanted to talk to him. She explained the details more than I was ready to do. They talked awhile, and then he wanted to talk with me again. He couldn't come over tonight, but he could come over tomorrow night, along with Robin. I thanked him, and we hung up.

Rosemary said she was also going to call Dr. John to fill him in before I would see him tomorrow. She was concerned I would be upset with her, but I thanked her for caring so much. She got out of my car and I drove home, thinking deeply about the whole situation. It was embarrassing to share my weaknesses so openly.

Wednesday, September 25, 2013

I awoke this morning feeling shaky. It was Bible study morning, and I was trying to calm down for that, but it wasn't working. I was near tears and not feeling very functional.

When the group showed up, I could tell Fr. Pat was checking on me. I found it difficult to concentrate on the study, and I was doing more daydreaming than listening.

The group left, and I sat in the living room, deep in thought, until my session with Dr. John. I couldn't fight the shakiness I was feeling. I walked into Dr. John's office already feeling the tears in my eyes. I told him how I had cut my wrist with a razor blade yesterday, and how shaky I was feeling. I knew some of my nervousness was building because of Rebecca's wedding this coming weekend. It would be so special to see my godchild get married, but I also knew it would stir up memories of my own wedding. And Bill.

I gave a full account to Dr. John about the previous day's problems and my worries about keeping it together at Rebecca's wedding. I could see he was concerned for me and was listening carefully. When the session was over, he told me to call him the next day or two so he could see how I was doing.

Back home, I called my therapist to tell her I wouldn't be coming to group this evening. I felt too shaky to deal with participating in a group, but more important, Fr. Pat and his wife Robin were coming to my house to talk. Again I sat alone for a while, thinking about how the talk with Fr. Pat would be.

Fr. Pat and Robin arrived, and I again felt embarrassed. I wasn't used to sharing my thoughts and feelings so intimately, and I wasn't sure how much I would be able to talk with them. But of highest importance to me was not losing my intimacy with God, so talking with Fr. Pat was important to me.

Fr. Pat let me know he had thought deeply and prayed about our conversation tonight. He told me how concerned they are about me and reinforced that I'm much loved by them and by my church family. But then the tough love started. He said, "If Bill is watching you while you hurt yourself, it would be a disgrace to his memory."

That hurt to hear, but I had already thought about that, so it didn't have a lot of shock value. I believe Bill is in Heaven, so he understands just how much pain I'm in. I don't feel my actions could hurt him in any way.

After that we settled down to a calmer tone of conversation, which helped me to talk about what I'm going through. As they were leaving, we exchanged hugs. I felt worn out after our talk, even though it had helped in some ways. I went to bed exhausted.

Thursday, September 26, 2013

I felt shaky when I got out of bed this morning, but less shaky than the night before. I spent the day trying to do more weed pulling in my yard. I was tired, so again I would work for a while, take a break, and do some more. As the day went on, I was feeling a little calmer, and I felt ready to face the Thursday night Bible study.

Everyone arrived, including Fr. Pat and Robin. Father gave me a hug so I knew he was checking on how I was doing. This time I was able to concentrate a little better during the scripture reading. And after the session was over, Father stopped to give me another hug. Yes, I knew he cared.

Friday, September 27, 2013

Rebecca's wedding weekend is drawing near. Gary, father of the bride, brought her dog, Porter, over to my house for the weekend. Porter and Lady had met a few times before, so I wasn't worried about how they would act together. And they started off just fine. Porter will be at my house until Sunday, when I'll bring him back to Beth's house. Beth and Gary will keep Porter until the honeymoon is was over.

Saturday, September 28, 2013

Becky's big day. I did a little yard work again, hoping that would relax me some. I was very grateful that Julie, my step-daughter, and her husband were picking me up for the wedding, especially because the wedding was downtown. I don't even like to see the skyline of downtown anymore, because it was the location of Bill's work accident.

It took quite a while for me to get ready; it's been such a long time since I got dressed up for anything. It was uncomfortable to be getting ready by myself, without Bill, so I kept focusing on Julie and Bob being with me soon.

We arrived at the hall, which would house both the wedding and the reception. They had picked an old factory/ business building that had been renovated into hall space. It gave it an Old World charm along with a new, worldly sophistication. Rebecca had chosen well.

The wedding was lovely, the dinner a delight, and then the dancing began. I knew this was going to be the hardest part. Bill and I had loved to dance, and I've not yet been able to listen to music without thinking about him. Everyone was, of course, jumping up to dance, and there I was at the table with a note taped on my forehead that read "Widow." I got teary-eyed again and tried to hold it in. After a while, Rebecca came over to the table with me and showed me some much-needed attention. What a sweet godchild I have—it gave me a little boost. She and I even got up to dance together.

Soon Julie and Bob were talking about leaving, because they were going to pick up their baby. I was grateful; I had heard enough music and seen enough dancing. I was glad to be going home.

Sunday, September 29, 2013

Gift opening day. I didn't feel like moving off the couch, but yesterday I had kept Becky's dog at my house because the wedding party and family had stayed at a downtown hotel. Today I would be bringing Porter over to Beth's house. The family was gathering for the gift opening, and giving well wishes to the just-married couple on their way to their honeymoon. I looked like most of them: tired. And that was okay.

A short afternoon, and I headed home. I sat on the couch for the rest of the day, tired but with an active mind, thinking about all that had happened in the past week.

Monday, September 30, 2013

I went to Diana's office today for my therapy session. We discussed the previous week, and I let her know how shaky so much of it had been. I also explained that I'd had a talk with Fr. Pat and Robin, and how the talk had in some ways been good, but also tough to hear.

I left the session still feeling tired, but pleased that I didn't have any other plans for the day.

Tuesday, October 1, 2013

Yeah, again no plans today. And yes, self-isolation is where I'm headed. I just want to think about Bill, with no interruptions.

Wednesday, October 2, 2013

After today's session with Dr. John started, I could see how his serious questions were searching for how I was doing. I was still very tense and tired, but I thought I was starting, just a little, to relax. He asked if I had any activities planned, but that was a big fat zero. I told him isolating was big on my list. I knew he wasn't too happy about that.

Saturday, October 19, 2013

I'm meeting with Beth this morning. It's been a long time since we've been able to get together on a Saturday. She had a very busy summer, with Rebecca getting married in September.

We decided to check out some rummage sales and, as usual, I got a couple of things. I still felt a little nervous with her, since she was so upset with me when I called her from the psych hospital. It's good that we are back to talking as friends.

Sunday, October 20, 2013

My church, Holy Cross Anglican Church, has temporarily moved to share a church building with a Lutheran church that has only twelve members. Today is the first mass I'll be attending there. I'm glad for the change, because we'll be meeting in a real church again, not just a classroom. I hope to feel at home here soon. I need that.

I'm still having problems with nervousness when I go to the cemetery to visit Bill. And I still don't know exactly why. I sob so hard when I go there; I think it's because my emotions are raw. I envision Bill lying below where I'm sitting, and I guess it validates that he's gone. And I can't admit that yet.

Instead of going to the cemetery today, I headed home, feeling exhausted. I sat down in my living room and just thought about Bill.

Monday, October 21, 2013

I'm feeling edgy today. I had my appointment with Diana, and our conversations often get me wound up. She lays out what she thinks, which is good because I don't want small talk; I want someone to get me thinking. But at times she is so blunt that I get the feeling I'm trapped in a corner. I think it's my own stubbornness.

I got home and already I wanted a drink. I'm thinking about our anniversary coming up on Saturday, and it reminds me of our wedding day. That makes me cry.

Tuesday, October 22, 2013

I'm still feeling edgy, but it helped having coffee with Rosemary today. I can talk about anything with my widow friend. She asked me many questions about how I was doing and if I wanted any companionship on Bill's and my wedding anniversary. She said she'd be glad to help. I thanked her, but said no; I was already planning out my day.

I would buy a bottle of champagne similar to the kind we had on our wedding day. I would fill both of our wedding glasses and see if I would be able to think about our special day.

I also decided to go to the cemetery at the time of the wedding ceremony. I remembered my thoughts from last Sunday, when I wanted to visit the cemetery but was too afraid to go because I knew it would be terribly difficult. I had been thinking about sitting on the ground and, unfortunately, I had been picturing how Bill would look now. It made me mad to think that way, but the images would just pop into my mind. I prayed, hoping that would help me think instead about where Bill's soul is now.

Wednesday, October 23, 2013

I was glad to see Dr. John today. My nerves have been getting worse, and seeing him usually calms me down some. At today's session, he asked about Saturday being my wedding anniversary. I started crying and told him I wasn't doing very well. He said that I could go into the hospital if I wasn't able to handle this. I told him I didn't want to. He reminded me that I should come to the hospital or call him if I had any thoughts of harming myself. I appreciated his thoughtfulness.

Thursday, October 24, 2013

I spent the day trying to accomplish some things, both inside and outside of my house. But I didn't get very far. My thoughts about our wedding day were increasing, and that was tiring me. I felt exhausted after doing almost anything. I gave up and tried to find something to watch on TV. That didn't work either. My thoughts were turned inward.

Friday, October 25, 2013

I was almost too weary to climb the steps to the second floor to see my therapist, Ken. My body was hurting all over. I was fighting the urge to start crying. I knew my emotions were causing my body to ache and feel exhausted, too.

When Ken came to get me from the waiting room, I was near tears. I sat down in his office, and finally the tears came. I could see Ken was nervous listening to me, while I cried and tried to explain how I wanted to die. He suggested I go into the hospital, but again I said no. He also reminded me to come to the hospital if I had thoughts of harming myself. We talked for a while, but I had trouble concentrating.

When I got home, I had an early drink that caused me to be drowsy for the rest of the day. By the time I went to bed that evening, trying to fall asleep, my mind was whirling with thoughts of our wedding rehearsal and the rehearsal dinner. I remembered being so excited that whole day—it was the start to my new life. My life as Bill's wife. I had never felt so wonderful. At the church, the priest gave us directions on what to do. I felt so giddy that I was talking to Beth and not listening to the priest. Bill kept shushing us, reminding me to listen, but for some reason I just couldn't do it. I was too excited.

The next day I learned my lesson, because I wasn't sure what to do. Luckily, Bill was much more learned about church ceremonies. He had listened to the priest, and he showed me what to do. And he had fun telling that story through the years, getting everyone to chuckle at me.

I knew these thoughts were increasing my tension, but I didn't know how to block them out. After some effort, I finally fell asleep.

Saturday, October 26, 2013

I awoke, and immediately felt the deep sadness of this anniversary day. *How has everything changed so much?* I questioned. Our once busy house was horribly quiet. Thank goodness I could still hear Lady's morning reminder, a bark every few seconds, to get me up. At least there was Lady to talk to.

I got up, took Lady out and fed her, and took my morning pills. Then I sat down in an easy chair in the living room. I just sat there, listening to the silence of our house, for a long time, until I checked the clock to see if it was nearing 2:00 p.m.— the time of our wedding. It was time for my planned drive to the cemetery.

I dreaded the drive, not anticipating this visit. And I felt guilty that I was dreading it. For four years I had gone to the cemetery nearly every Sunday after church. It had felt like the right thing to do. It was only recently that I had grown scared of going there. But I wasn't going to chicken out today because I felt I should be there.

I parked and walked toward his gravesite, feeling the tears welling in my eyes. I stood next to Bill's plot; it was too cold for me to sit on the ground. I prayed and I talked with Bill, with more tears forming and threatening to spill over. I glanced at the headstone, noticing for the first time that it was slightly askew, as if it had been pushed or bumped by something. I looked at the grass, and it was newly cut. I instantly felt angry—the person cutting the grass must have hit Bill's headstone. I tried to remind myself to call the cemetery office on Monday.

After that severe change of thought, from Bill to the headstone, I decided I had been there long enough and walked back to the car to head home.

I cried again as I drove home. *Everything feels so lonely all the time*, I thought. *There's no day-to-day happiness anymore. Just sadness.* I knew my depression was increasing again and gaining a hold on me. It felt like the devil was grabbing at my arm. I knew I needed to pray more, to ask God to help me through all of this. But when I got depressed, it was hard to concentrate on prayer. That, again, was the devil. I learned to tell the devil, in the name of God, to get away from me. That helped me feel better.

Entering my house, I again thanked God for my dog Lady. There she was, wagging her tail, meeting me at the door, so happy that I was back home. I couldn't imagine going on without her. She stayed by my side constantly. At times I felt bad because whenever I moved from one room to another, she followed me, lying down where I sat. I would move to another room, and she would get up to follow me again. Her arthritis made it difficult to get up, so I felt guilty that I was making her move so much. But again, maybe the constant movement helped keep the arthritis from getting worse.

I sat in the living room staring out the window, with Lady at my side, resting a bit before having my champagne toast. But it was on my mind, so I headed for the china cabinet to get our wedding goblets. During our engagement, as we were filling out our gift registration, Bill saw these goblets and decided that these were it. I was so touched that he would think of something like that. And they were beautiful. We took them home right away.

I filled two goblets with champagne and thought of Bill as I began to sip wine from each goblet. I felt close to Bill, and I hoped he was with me. I knew he would be enjoying the moment. Amazingly, I finished the bottle quite fast. And surprisingly I didn't feel much of a buzz. I was disappointed; I wanted to be drunk to help me through this day.

I went back to the living room and sat back in the lounge chair. I soon found out the champagne was working after all: I was asleep in seconds, only to wake up an hour later. I guess it did have an effect on me. When I awoke, I felt so depressed that I couldn't stand it. I sat there holding my favorite wedding picture of us. It was during our vows, and Bill and I were standing facing each other. Our eyes were fixed on each other, and each of us wore a slight smile, showing just how happy we were at that moment. I held that picture close to my chest, trying to feel Bill's presence.

I suddenly realized I'd forgot about taking my pills. I took them and sat down in the lounge chair again, drifting in and out of sleep. Thinking about Bill. Holding that picture. And then I heard a hello at my side door. Robin had come over, bringing me some soup and a DVD of *Gone with the Wind*. She gave me a sweet smile, as if she was trying to bring me some cheer but trying not to be too cheery.

She asked if I wanted to watch the movie. I've always wanted to be alone on our wedding anniversary, but somehow the thought of a long movie that I loved interested me. And, somehow, Clark Gable had always reminded me a bit of Bill. So that interested me more. We put the DVD in.

I wasn't sure how difficult it would be to watch a movie today, so I went and made myself a drink. I was again trying to numb my emotions. And I think we both forgot just how long the movie was. Four hours later, a tired Robin was ready to go home to Fr. Pat. I was happy that I also felt so tired that I could go straight to bed. The movie had worked; I was ready for sleep.

After Robin left, I let Lady out for the night and headed to bed. Amazingly, I was asleep before I knew it. Thank God—and thank Robin.

Sunday, October 27, 2013

I awoke with my alarm buzzing, very annoyingly. Fortunately I had remembered the night before to set my alarm. After mass, Fr. Pat always asked if anyone was celebrating any birthdays or anniversaries, so I planned to walk up to the front of the church, holding my picture of Bill and me taking our vows. I was afraid I would be crying, but I still wanted to do it. I took care of my morning chores for Lady, got dressed, and headed for church.

I sat in my normal place in the back of the church, trying to calm my fragile nerves. Robin came and sat with me. She said she always sits with her boys, but today she wanted to sit with me—so sweet. The mass began, and I concentrated on that.

At the end of the mass, as the recessional song began, I soon knew what song it was: one we had picked for our wedding. It wasn't played often, so I was amazed that it was being played on our anniversary weekend. I immediately wanted to sing along, but tears were pouring down my checks. Robin put her arm around me and told me that Bill was here, singing along with us. That was exactly what I had hoped for.

The song ended, and we sat while Fr. Pat headed back up the aisle to the front of the church. There it was—he was asking about birthdays and anniversaries. I picked up my picture and headed to the altar. Father saw I had the picture and said a prayer for us. He gave me a hug, and I headed back to my seat. I was exhausted, but I had done what I had set out to do.

Afterward, everyone headed toward the back of the church, where we had our coffee and conversation time. This wasn't the day for me to participate, so I headed out to my car. I had done it, and I felt proud. I felt close to Bill. But now I just wanted to head back home. Back to Lady and my lounge chair.

Monday, October 28, 2013

Today I saw Diana and told her about my emotional weekend. I still felt shaky about the whole thing and broke down in her office. But soon we were talking; she asked me questions and offered her ideas. She was good to talk with. I felt a little better by the time I left.

Tuesday, October 29, 2013

I was pretty lazy all day. I think I was still exhausted because of the weekend. I tried to do a little inside the house, but I didn't get very far. I was once again sitting in my chair in the living room when I saw a truck pull into my driveway. I couldn't imagine who that would be. I saw a man get out, so I went to the door. To my large surprise, Tommy was at the door.

Tommy was my friend Dave's nephew and Tom's son. Tommy had been a part of our team of contractors, who had worked on our previous rectory project. Dave, Tommy, and I were quite a team. We worked hard, and we enjoyed each other's company. When we finished that project, Tommy found another job, and I didn't see him for quite a while.

So here was Tommy again, after all this time. I sadly guessed that he wanted money, but I still was glad to see him. He looked very nervous when I greeted him and let him in. We sat on the couch, and I asked him what was up. He told me he had stopped at the rectory to see Fr. Sam, not knowing that we had lost the church, and Fr. Sam was no longer our rector. A woman had answered the door and told Tommy that Fr. Sam wasn't there anymore.

So Tommy decided to come to me. He asked if there were things I would like to get done around the house, so I knew he needed money. But I took it slow.

He told me his story. He confirmed that the last time I saw him he and his fiancée had been using drugs. But he said they had stopped over a year ago, and they were both in treatment for drug abuse. Once again, they were both out of work, and if they didn't pay their rent by the end of the month (in two days) they would be evicted.

As I listened, I thought, *Is he telling me the truth?* And even if he was telling me the truth, it didn't mean that he wouldn't disappear once he got the money. I thought about their three kids. I felt terrible for them, and I knew what I was going to do.

I told Tommy I would help him out and hire him if he would join the Bible study group and try out my church. I came up with this idea because he and his fiancée had both told me previously that they wanted to start going to church. And Tommy used to attend Bible study back when Fr. Sam had taught it.

Tommy jumped at that idea. He said he really wanted to try it. Again, my thoughts were, *Will he follow through on this?* It was so sad not knowing. I gave him money for rent and told him to be here in the morning for Bible study and, afterward, work.

Wednesday, October 30, 2013

Wow, Tommy showed up for Bible study! I found that amazing. And he seemed to enjoy it. He was listening and taking notes.

After Bible study I was ready to put him to work. I had been trying to get the rest of the mulch off my patio and front yard before it started snowing. When he was ready to leave, I reminded him, if possible, to come to Thursday's Bible study. That wasn't in the deal, but it'd be the only time his fiancée would be able to come. Amazingly, she had just been accepted for a job—and better yet, a good job.

Thursday, October 31, 2013

Bible study began and ended. No Tommy or Melissa. I felt the feeling of failure creeping in. I hoped not.

Friday, November 1, 2013

Tommy showed up this morning. Oh, that felt good. He had to bring along his daughter because she was only three. His two boys were in school, so he would need to leave by 3:30 p.m. to pick them up. That meant he would be working half days, and that was fine with me.

Saturday, November 2, and Sunday, November 3, 2013

My deal with Tommy was only for Monday through Friday. He has plenty of work at home to be done—and he needs to see his kids. That's okay; I figured I would like the days off too.

Monday, November 4, 2013

Tommy showed up again for work. I think I'm going to like this. I started a list of things he could do, because if I just told him, one of us would forget. I had already hired someone to mow the lawn and pick up the leaves, but Tommy would need to clean out the gutters. Thank goodness I had worked this all out. The first year that Bill was gone, I tried raking the leaves by myself, and I cried at how hard it was alone. Luckily, Billy and Julie (my step kids), and Scott and Debbie (my brother and sister-in-laws), helped me with the next time the trees lost their leaves. That helped immensely. They did it the following years also, but I knew I needed to find someone permanent to do it. And I did!

Friday, November 8, 2013

The week has gone well. Tommy showed up for Bible study and for work all week. It's a good start. Of course as soon as Roger and Beth heard about it, the red flags went up. They were both worried about me, since they don't know him very well. They told me to keep my eyes open; I was doing that anyway.

Saturday, November 9, 2013 and Sunday, November 10, 2013

As the first week of November ended, I started thinking about the rest of the month, which included my birthday and Thanksgiving. I would prefer to skip them both, but there's no way around it. They both are very emotional for me. And then there's Christmas—without Bill. Every second reminded me of the hole his sudden death left in our family.

As usual, I would need to take it step by step.

Monday, November 11, 2013

Tommy called this morning to say he wouldn't be able to come to work today. He had some errands he had to take care of. I didn't mind that, as long as he called.

Tuesday, November 12, 2013

All is well—Tommy was back at work today, along with his daughter, Jorja (yes, that's how they spell it). She's a darling little thing, but her curiosity is great. Somehow the house doesn't look quite the same after she leaves. But it's so cute watching her follow her dad around. She wants to help him with everything that he lets her do.

Friday, November 15, 2013

Another week done. Tommy's a hard worker, but I have to remind him to stick to the list. If he sees something that needs to be fixed, it's not unusual for him to stop what he's doing and start working on that. I actually do like that, because I don't know about all the things that are broken.

He's also not afraid to do anything. When he comes around mid-morning, one of the first things he does is clean up the kitchen. I love that—it hasn't happened since Mom was here.

Saturday, November 16, 2013

When we have time, Beth and I usually get together on Saturday mornings. But not this one. I had my widows' group to go to, and Beth has a lot going on with the fall leaves and the final fall clean-up chores in her yard. I wish my yard was as clean as hers.

Yard work is on my list for Monday. Not this afternoon. My heart isn't in it today. And I'll probably be tired after the widows' group. They'll probably have some holiday theme, and that will make me emotional again.

Sunday, November 17, 2013

I made it to church as usual this morning. Next I thought about going to the cemetery, but I'm just not up to that yet. I headed home instead, telling Bill I was sorry.

Monday, November 18, 2013

Today my project was to lay newspaper down on my weeds and then put mulch around my plants and on top of the newspaper. I decided to have Tommy wheelbarrow the mulch to me. That was a lot of work off my hands. I don't think I would've lasted more than two loads.

By the end of the day, we got a lot done, but it's going to take another couple of days to finish it.

Well, I was wrong about another couple of days. I have plenty left to do, but I told Tommy just to make a leftover pile of the mulch for next year. It's getting too cold to do this anymore till spring. And I've been seeing snowflakes in the air. Time to go inside and light a fire in the downstairs fireplace.

Bill used to do most of the firewood labor. He would bring it home from someplace (usually the dump) in such large pieces that I would yell at him for carrying too much. But he would get them out of the trailer and start using his chainsaw and wood splitter on them. Then he had to wheel them to our oversized basement window well, where we would throw them down the chute. It was really quite a good system he had built—much better than walking them downstairs in a wood carrier, and much nicer for the walls that used to get nicked up all over the place.

After Bill passed, Billy helped at first with getting wood, but then he moved to Texas. I'm worried about how I'm going to get more wood now. But at least Tommy loads up the existing wood and dumps it down the chute.

Thursday, November 21, 2013

I was never a big birthday person, but now I don't care for them at all. Without Bill sitting next to me, I feel awfully lonely. But Beth has created a new diversion for me: there's a Mexican restaurant not far from our homes, so we go there— with Roger and Terry following soon afterward—and we all have supper. Beth knows that I can't turn down Mexican food.

Friday, November 22, 2013

Tommy took the day off, which was fine for me. I'm still tired from celebrating last night, so I had today planned out—to be lazy. I learned lazy from Bill. He actually was a hard-working man, but when he just didn't feel like doing anything, he would sit down in his easy chair downstairs, turn on the TV, and with clicker in hand, watch whatever he felt like watching—mostly news shows he had taped for himself. He knew I didn't care about watching a news show a day late, so that was fine with me. We would tease him that he was lazy, but he'd get a grin on his face like he was proud of it. I found it quite cute. And I would usually end up joining him.

Saturday, November 23, 2013

I got a wonderful call from Shannon, my other daughter-in-law. She and her husband Paul have decided to host Thanksgiving at their house. That's great! No preparing the turkey, no cleaning up. I just have to make the pumpkin and apple pies, which is hard enough. Bill loved those pies and usually sat with me while I was getting them ready the day before. But I think overall this will make the day emotionally easier for me. If I have trouble emotionally, I can go hide in the bathroom for a while.

Thursday, November 28, 2013—Thanksgiving Day

Scott, Debbie, and the kids drove me to Paul and Shannon's house, which was a real help. I was right—it was difficult making those pies, but not as difficult as making the whole dinner. I still struggled, but it felt more like a party than Thanksgiving, and that was also helping. Hope we do it there again next year.

Sunday, December 1, 2013

The first day of December. There's some snow on the ground, and neighbors have put up their outside Christmas lights. It's officially Christmas season. Now to figure out how to get through the month. November was rough enough, but December?

Thank goodness, Beth promised to help me get some of my presents, so now to set a date with her.

Monday, December 2, 2013

I had coffee with Rosemary this morning. Rosemary has words worth gold. Whether I'm down in the dumps or holding my own, she always has something to say that's worth hearing, especially when I'm emotional. She has a way of showing such concern. She won't let up unless I prove I'll be okay. And she'll be ready to get on the phone with either Dr. John or Fr. Pat if she thinks more help is needed. And she will end it all with a prayer that warms my spirit. I love our meetings. Usually by the end of the conversation she has lifted my heart and put a smile on my face.

Tuesday, December 3, 2013

Unfortunately those smiles don't last too long. I had my appointment with my therapist, Diana, this afternoon, and I had to admit to her that I'm not doing very well. This whole holiday season is already getting to me. I'm feeling a lot of anxiety and crying much more. I've also been drinking some again. She's never happy when she hears something like that.

"At least I got through Thanksgiving without too much of a hitch," I told her, "but it seems to be weighing on me now."

There's no hint of Christmas at my house yet. I'm not ready for it.

Wednesday, December 4, 2013

Today I saw Dr. John. I pretty much told him the same story I told Diana yesterday. That's often helpful because of the different comments and opinions they offer me. Dr. John was concerned about how I was going to get through this whole Christmas season. He said I should drop some of the old holiday traditions and focus on something besides the holiday. Easier said than done, when every light in the city is flashing green and red—even the stop lights. He told me to wait until next week and see how I'm doing. I wish I had more time to talk with him.

Friday, December 6, 2013

And today I saw Ken. We talked for a while about having to give things up. His favorite comparison was that he had a bad back and had to give up golf. He wasn't comparing his story to mine, but he was trying to explain that things we like eventually go away, no matter how trivial or important they are. I like Ken because he's very spiritual and often talks about the Bible and faith. That suits me fine.

Saturday, December 7, 2013

Today Beth and I went shopping. I tried to get simple presents as much as possible. And if I didn't know what to get, Beth was great at coming up with ideas—she's always like that. So I got quite a bit done and want to get the rest soon. I don't want to be in busy stores at the last minute. That would be too hard.

Friday, December 13, 2013

Bill's birthday. Tommy did some work around the house, but all I felt like doing was thinking about Bill. Just like my birthday, Bill's birthday was never that important to him, but we would always have a family gathering for him. He actually made a pretty funny birthday boy—with his funny faces and taking forever to read his cards and open his presents. It showed how much everyone cared about him, and I think he really enjoyed the celebration.

Monday, December 16, 2013

I decided Christmas was getting pretty close, so with list in hand, I went out to get the rest of the presents I needed to get. I wasn't happy about it, but it had to be done. Luckily some were gift certificates for Billy's Texas bunch, and others were in just a couple of stores. That made it easier, even though I was a tense mess.

Tuesday, December 17, 2013

When Tommy showed up for work, I asked him if we could get a Christmas tree for me. He said that would be fine. I found a tree right away, which is what I wanted—a quick in and out. Tommy put up the tree in the stand, and I let him know that all the Christmas boxes in the basement would need to be brought upstairs. I thanked him profusely; that was a lot off my mind.

I also called Shannon to see if they could come over on Thursday night. I wanted Shannon and the kids, Jessica and Erik, to help decorate, and I wanted Jessica to build the Christmas village that I used to make every year. She agreed, and I let out a sigh of relief. God is watching out for me.

Wednesday, December 18, 2013

My visit with Dr. John was a bit rough. I was very nervous, anxious, and crying. I could see the concern in Dr. John's eyes. But we decided to wait another week and see how I'm doing.

Thursday, December 19, 2013

While I was gone, Tommy and Melissa brought up all the boxes and decorated the tree for me. I couldn't believe it when I got home—the tree was done. I was thrilled that I didn't have to see it being done, or worse yet, have to do it myself. That would have been very depressing for me. Tommy and Melissa were so much help that I couldn't believe it. The houses for the Christmas village were still in their boxes for Jessica to build the village tonight.

By the time Shannon and the kids came, everything was ready for them. I thanked God for everyone helping me.

Friday, December 20, 2013

Today I saw Ken. After listening to me for a while and watching me cry, he suggested that maybe I should go into the hospital again. The thought of that was impossible. I have to get through Christmas first. Everyone is coming to my house. I just can't cancel it, especially for the grandkids. I said no.

Saturday, December 21, 2013

I am emotionally exhausted from yesterday. I spent today fixing up a few things, but I also spent quite a lot of time in my lounge chair again.

Sunday, December 22, 2013

At church, I felt especially emotional. I sang the songs, remembering how Bill would always sing them with such joy. He sang loudly and proudly, pronouncing each word like you knew he really meant it. I drove home and sobbed for a long time.

Once I was through with that, I pulled out all of the presents and started wrapping or bagging them. I had to cluster them by family to make sure I hadn't forgotten anything. With that done, I started a list for groceries I'll need. I'm going to ask Tommy to go with me tomorrow.

Monday, December 23, 2013

Tommy said he'd be happy to help me grocery shop, so we went right away. I was most worried about the ham. I didn't want to find out they didn't have any large ones left. But it was no problem; I got everything I needed.

Tuesday, December 24, 2013 — Christmas Eve

Christmas Eve was at my house, like it has been for years. We had dinner first, and then we opened presents. It was pretty rough on me, but I tried hard not to show it. I didn't want to ruin Christmas for anyone else. They all had plenty of years of enjoyment left in life, and I didn't want to cause any sorrow for them.

Wednesday, December 25, 2013 — Christmas Day

First I went to church, which was heartbreaking. Singing the Christmas songs without Bill was tremendously difficult. I tried to hold back my tears, but they came anyway. I left shortly after church ended and headed home. I felt very tired from a short night's sleep and all the tension I was holding inside.

Christmas Day in the past was mostly just for Bill and me. Once in a while one of the kids would stop by, but otherwise it was Bill and me, being lazy, listening to Christmas music, and eating leftover ham and pie. With all of those memories, it was excruciating being home alone. And I had given all the leftovers to the family, since I knew I wouldn't be able to enjoy them by myself. I was very depressed and didn't know what to do about it. So I tried to sleep while watching TV. At least this way the day would go faster.

I also stopped by Beth's house to give them their presents. I didn't stay long because I was too depressed, but I did tell Beth I was going into the hospital. She had never seemed happy about my hospitalizations, because I had been in there before and I wasn't any better, as she saw it. I let her know that being in the hospital did calm me down, so that was something.

Later in the evening I did have a nice visit from Roger and Terry. Terry always spends the day with her family, so Roger came first and Terry showed up later. I was glad to have them here, but I couldn't hide how I was feeling. We had a nice visit, though, even when they knew I was sad.

Thursday, December 26, 2013

Today, when I saw Dr. John, I was in such a deep depression that I felt I could hardly talk. Dr. John grew very concerned about me when I started talking about drinking and suicide again. He decided I needed to be admitted right away. I'm dreading that, but I also feel so lifeless that I know it's probably for the best.

I have some things I have to wrap up before I go into the hospital, so I agreed to go in on Sunday night. I have to check with Roger about caring for Lady while I'm gone, and I have to ask Tommy about taking down my Christmas decorations. I'll talk with them tomorrow.

Friday, December 27, 2013

I called Roger to tell him what's going on and to wish him a happy birthday. Like me, he doesn't enjoy celebrating his birthday anymore, but I somehow always manage to sneak in a "Happy birthday!" wish. He agreed to take Lady; as usual, he'll pick her up on Monday so I can spend my last night before hospitalization with her.

Saturday, December 28, 2013

I spent my last day at home alone and crying a lot. I felt so terribly depressed. I was missing Lady even though she hadn't yet left with Roger. I tried to read but with no success. I just sat in my chair, flipping stations on the TV.

I remembered to call Tommy, and I told him what's going on. He said he'll be happy to help take down the Christmas things. I also told him he could continue to do whatever work was to be done on my "to do" list. And, if it snowed, he would be doing the shoveling. That eased my mind a lot. I would be glad to come back home with all of those things already done. Tommy was indeed a Godsend.

Sunday, December 29, 2013

I couldn't get myself to go to church this morning. I for sure didn't want to talk about going into the hospital. So I sat with Lady most of the day, trying to give her attention so hopefully she won't worry about me too much. I love that dog so much.

Later this evening I packed my bag and left for the hospital, planning to leave my car in the parking lot there again. I'm a little worried that if we have a lot of snow my car could be buried, but then I can call Tommy to help me clear it out.

It's become my routine to go into the hospital late on a Sunday night. Dr. John doesn't do rounds on Sundays, and not much is going on, so I try to get there late; that way, I can go right to bed after intake. On Monday, everyone comes back and it's busy.

Once again, I found myself walking the hallway toward the intake desk. There were just a couple of other people before me, but I wasn't in any hurry anyway. Paperwork completed, interview completed, and I was on my way to the unit for processing. Again they searched me and my bag. I was learning most of the things I shouldn't bring. They would just lock them up anyway. But I always had my purse, so they always locked that up.

Finally, I was in my room and alone. And able to go to sleep.

Monday, December 30, 2013

My first day after intake, as expected was very busy. All the staff—nurses, medical doctor, case manager, therapist, and Dr. John—came to see me. I felt depressed and exhausted. I slept the rest of the morning and then started my afternoon group sessions.

Tuesday, December 31, 2013—New Year's Eve

I started to settle in. I noticed this time, since I was seeing most of the same people, that my talks with them weren't quite as long. I'm disappointed in this; part of the reason I'm here is to discuss what is bothering me. Maybe they feel like they already knew my story. But I don't care; I want to talk about it.

It's strange being in the hospital on New Year's Eve. One of the therapists took on the role of planning some games to celebrate. I didn't want any part of this, so I went to my room to be alone. All I could think about was the New Year's Eve party that Bill and I had gone to just after he proposed to me. Now here I am, sitting on a hospital bed, crying. Life sure has changed.

Wednesday, January 1, through Thursday, January 9, 2014

Even though I was here for almost two weeks, it seemed like the time went fast. Sort of a blur. I began to wonder if my medications were too strong for me, but I didn't want to say anything because at the same time they might be helping me.

It was quite a boring time. I never met any other patients that I could converse with. My nurses and therapist didn't really spend much time talking with me. I think my deep depression gave an appearance of *stay away from me*.

I attended all of my sessions, but nothing really pertained to me that helped me. It might have been that I wasn't listening attentively. I guess the best thing that happened was that I calmed down some. My anniversary was over, the holidays were over; that was a relief. I was relaxing more, with no deadlines to meet, besides what was happening in the hospital.

Later one night toward the end of my stay, after I had gone to bed, I awoke and realized I had to go to the bathroom. I had forgotten to leave the bathroom light on, which meant my room was pitch dark, so I decided to take it slow. That didn't help;

somehow I caught my foot on the chair leg. Instead of falling straight down, like I should have, I grabbed the bathroom door handle and tried to hold on. That didn't work, so my arm was pulled pretty hard. I could really feel the pain. In fact, in the position I was in, I also couldn't get up.

I hated to do it, but I had to start yelling for help. Quickly the nurses came in and helped me get up and got me into bed. I told them how much my arm hurt, and they felt it to see if it was broken. They didn't think so, and we all decided it was probably a sprain. So I went back to sleep.

Saturday, January 11, 2014

Dr. John talked with me this morning and said he felt it was best that I be discharged. He wants me to go into the Intensive Outpatient Program (IOP) because the sessions might do me some good. I'm not happy about this, but once again he wasn't asking me, he was telling me. I'll be starting on Monday, January 13th.

I drove to Roger's house to get Lady. I don't know which of us was happier. I stayed a while and then headed home. I was ecstatic to find the house emptied of Christmas stuff. And it was perfectly clean. Thank you, Tommy and Melissa.

Sunday, January 12, 2014

I made sure I went to church today. I needed direction from God on how to live my life. Everything lately has been so hard. It's time for me to listen to God and stop trying to take the lead. Once again I'm reminded that I should be doing His will, not mine.

Monday, January 13, 2014

During the IOP I won't be seeing my therapists, but I'll still be seeing Dr. John once a week. Dr. John is hoping the IOP will help me stop using alcohol as a means to numb my pain. He has told me countless times that the alcohol isn't letting the medications work properly. I told him I stopped using alcohol, but he's worried I'll start again, which I often do.

I didn't like the IOP session today. I was bored. The class was mostly full of alcoholics and drug addicts, and I didn't relate to any of them. The class was explaining all about alcohol, but I didn't need to hear that either. I don't crave alcohol; I use it to numb my pain.

Thursday, January 16, 2014

In the morning I had my IOP session, and in the afternoon I had my appointment with Dr. John. I complained to him that I didn't want to continue the IOP. He said he still wants me to go, that it might help some, and that it only lasts for two weeks. Once again I said okay.

Wednesday, January 22, 2014

I saw Dr. John again. I know I'm not getting any better. I'm still deeply depressed, crying at most thoughts of Bill, and not concentrating well. Dr. John said we'll wait until next week to see if there are any changes.

Wednesday, January 29, 2014

Another weekly appointment with Dr. John. I was nervous to see him today because I had to explain to him that I had expected my last day in IOP would be January 23rd. When I told the therapist that the 23rd was my last day, she became annoyed and said the session was three weeks long, and if I left now, I wouldn't pass the class. I told her that didn't matter, my doctor had told me it was two weeks. And I left.

Dr. John said that I could go to the next session anyway, but I apologized and told him I couldn't stand the class and didn't want to go back. I knew he wasn't thrilled; he told me we would wait a week to see how I was.

I cried through most of today's session.

Friday, January 31, 2014

Late this morning, I met with Robin. That was enjoyable. She is nice to talk with, and it had been a long time since we had gotten together, especially because I've been in the hospital. It was probably one of the nicest visits I've experienced in the last few months.

Sunday, February 2, 2014

I went to church today, and it was a good thing, because we had a vestry meeting today. (Vestry refers to members selected by a congregation to conduct the business of a parish.) Since I've missed church so much lately, I wanted to make sure the vestry knew I was still interested in the position. I was still having trouble concentrating, but I tried as hard as I could to look okay.

Wednesday, February 12, 2014

Today was my appointment with Dr. John. I still feel like a mess, and I'm sure he could see that. He has decided I should go into the Partial Hospitalization Program again. I thought it was decided a while ago that I didn't have to go through it again, so I'm not happy about this news. He said we have to keep trying other things because he's seen no upward changes in me in some time.

Thursday, February 13, 2014

I hated hearing this news. I did partial about a year ago, and it didn't do much for me then. I had listened to the lectures and joined in the small group discussions. The best part was that Dr. John would come to see me each morning to check on how I was doing. I had a therapist assigned to me to see if I was making any progress. I knew my attitude then was all wrong, just like it is now—I'm being negative about everything, and I'm isolating as much as possible. I dread again having to go there five days a week, from 9:00 a.m. to 3:00 p.m., but the decision was made. I start tomorrow.

I'm also going to hate leaving Lady for so long, and I also hate leaving the house for that much time.

Friday, February 14, 2014

In the first day of partial today, I was diagnosed with suicidal ideation, urge to harm self, sad, tearful, worry, anxiety, grief, negative thoughts, social withdrawal, indecision, fear, and decreased energy. I think that about sums up everything I can think of.

Saturday, February 15, 2014

Another Key's Day. Each anniversary is so difficult to live through. They were such happy times, and now, nothing but tears. I'm glad it was on a Saturday so I didn't have to spend it in partial.

Sunday, February 16, 2014

After church I headed right home. I'm still not in the mood to talk with anyone. I'm very tense, especially in my stomach. I try to relax when this comes on, and I get the idea of having a drink. I'm trying not to do that.

My arm is still hurting after all this time. I decided I better go to my primary doctor to have it checked out.

Monday, February 17 to Friday, February 21, 2014

A full week of partial. I think I'm going to lose my mind. I listen and listen, but much of what I hear has nothing to do with me. Or I'm missing the parts that do concern me, out of boredom. I know I'm not cooperating enough, but I just can't seem to do it.

Friday, February 21, 2014

I made the big decision today. I asked to talk with my therapist at partial and told her I'm having such a hard time in these classes that I have to quit. She seemed concerned and cautioned me on just quitting. She said she would talk with my doctor. I apologized for the inconvenience, and I asked that she talk to him before Monday so he doesn't waste a trip over here.

Sunday, February 23, 2014

Today is my grandson Erik's birthday, and I was asked to make a pumpkin pie for the party. I don't know what it is about my in-laws, but many of them crave pumpkin pie. In fact, some of the kids don't like grocery store or restaurant pies anymore. It has to be the one that Grandma makes. But it's nice, because it's easy to make and I get compliments. That's good for my doldrums. It was also good to see most of the family. I don't see them very often anymore.

Wednesday, February 26, 2014

I was awfully nervous waiting for my session with Dr. John to start. Not only had I quit the IOP, now I had quit the partial program. I didn't want to know what he was going to say.

He came to get me, and sitting down in his office, there was a bit of silence at first. I explained how nervous and anxious I'd been in those classes and that I just couldn't sit in them anymore. Dr. John wasn't happy; I wasn't following his directions. He decided to leave it for a couple of weeks and see how I was doing.

Today I also had my appointment with my primary doctor. She looked at my shoulder and had an x-ray taken of it. She called me later to tell me the x-ray didn't show anything, but that I should see an orthopedic doctor and get an MRI for a better picture. I said I would do this, and she told me which doctor to see.

Friday, February 28, 2014

I had a session with Ken today. It had been a long time since I had seen him. We talked about what's been happening with me.

When I got home I made an appointment with the orthopedic doctor—for Monday. I was shocked to get in so quickly.

Later this evening the family threw a birthday party for Julie and Bob. Once again it was nice seeing everyone, but I felt very nervous at the bowling alley/bar, with music playing.

March 3, 2014

The orthopedic doctor checked out my arm and thinks I have a torn rotator cuff. I thought of Bill at once, since he had to go through that surgery twice. The doctor scheduled me for a couple weeks of physical therapy first, to see if it improves. If it doesn't improve, he's going to schedule me for an MRI before the surgery date is set.

How am I going to live my life with this injury? I can't believe this is happening from a simple fall.

Wednesday, March 5, 2014

Dr. John asked how I'm doing with my therapists, Ken and Diana. I told him I probably need more time with them. I told him about my shoulder, too. He decided to wait before doing anything else.

Friday, March 7, 2014

My session with Ken went okay. I think one problem I have is that he tells stories about himself or other patients, which I know is his way of connecting with me, but I don't always know if he's trying to make a point, or just trying to have a conversation. It sounds so selfish, but I want to talk about me, so I usually change the topic to how I'm feeling. I hope it will get better; I need to talk with him about it.

Monday, March 12, 2014

Following my discharge from partial, Dr. John decided I should start a two-week program called Mental Health IOP. They'll meet three times a week in the morning at the hospital grounds, beginning March 17th. From the way Dr. John described IOP, it sounded better than the other two programs. It's a smaller group so I should feel more comfortable.

Monday, March 17, 2014

I was nervous walking into my first day in the mental health IOP. I quickly learned that they discuss certain topics, and the group is asked to respond or ask questions as they want.

I mostly stayed quiet in the group, which is how I usually am. There aren't a lot of people in these groups who have just lost a spouse, so I usually listen for topics that pertain to me. The first session went pretty well.

I won't have any sessions with my therapist Diana until the IOP is completed, because both are on Mondays and insurance won't pay for two sessions in one day. It isn't a bad change of pace—and it's only for three weeks.

Tuesday, March 18, 2014

Today was my second session for the IOP. I'm feeling hopeful that I'll be comfortable in this group. Once again, I'll make an effort even though I still don't feel like I'm concentrating too well.

Wednesday, March 19, 2014

Today when I saw Dr. John, I told him I'm doing okay in the new IOP, and he looked thrilled. He reminded me that I should take it day to day and not try to rush anything. Then I reminded him that I'm going through physical therapy for my shoulder. The pain hasn't decreased, so it looks like I'll be having surgery to repair the torn rotator cuff.

Friday, March 21, 2014

I'm still seeing Ken, my regular therapist, because I don't have the IOP on Fridays. I'm glad of that—I want to keep some consistency in my week.

Thursday, March 27, 2014

Today was my last day of the new IOP. It was a small group session every day in which anyone could speak up. It felt good to be part of a group that I could tolerate. I feel like I learned some things, so it was worth it.

Friday, March 28, 2014

I hadn't seen Rosemary in quite a while, so it was nice to have lunch with her today. She always has a way of relaxing me. She completely understands what I'm going through, considering she lost her husband thirteen years ago. And her prayers are so sincere! How I wish I could pray like her.

Week of April 1, 2014

My weeks are really full now. I'll be back to seeing Diana soon, doing my physical therapy twice a week, attending Bible study twice a week, seeing Dr. John, seeing Ken—and somehow I snuck in seeing Robin for coffee. At least it's keeping me out of trouble.

Monday, April 7, 2014

My first appointment today was with Diana. I hadn't seen her for some time so it was a little hard to get back into it again. We mostly talked about my history this last month, and that pretty much filled up the session.

And today I saw the orthopedic surgeon. My MRI confirmed a torn rotator cuff, so surgery is set for April 24th. Definitely news I didn't want. He warned me that it entails a long recovery time, during much of the time I won't be able to drive. He also told me I'll be doing therapy for six to eight weeks, while I'm also doing therapy at home. This isn't going to be a small deal.

Tuesday, April 8, 2014

I told Tommy the bad news about my shoulder. I explained everything the surgeon had said and told him that I'm scared. I asked him if he would still be able to work for me—except now he would have to drive me to all my appointments and still handle any work that needs to be done around the house and yard. He wasn't happy for me, but at least he knew he'd still be working. And I was glad he said yes, or I don't know what I would have done.

Wednesday, April 9, 2014

Today I told Dr. John all about the surgery and aftercare. I explained how I had worked out the details with Tommy, so I should be able to attend all of my appointments. He felt bad that I have to go through this, but he was glad I had made some backup plans.

Saturday, April 12, 2014

Even though my shoulder hurts, I decided to attend the monthly widows' group. I wanted to tell a couple of the ladies what was going on in case I had to miss next month's meeting.

Sunday, April 13, 2014

Again, I'm glad I attended mass today because there was another vestry meeting. But yes, mass was more important. I have a lot of prayers to say before my surgery.

Wednesday, April 16, 2014

I had a pretty good session with Dr. John today. We talked about all the things I'm up against right now, and he encouraged me to not let them get me down. I still had trouble concentrating, and I was crying a lot, but not as bad as before.

Friday, April 18, 2014

Today's session with Ken was my last one before my surgery, so I reminded him that we shouldn't make any more appointments until I call him. He agreed and wished me luck.

Wednesday, April 21, 2014

I saw Diana today and told her this would be my last session with her until after the surgery. As with Ken, I reminded her that we shouldn't book any more appointments for now. She also agreed and wished me luck.

This afternoon I saw Dr. John and told him the same things. He told me to take care and he would see me soon.

I'm very nervous and scared about my surgery tomorrow.

Thursday, April 24, 2014, and

Friday, April 25, 2014

Fortunately I had to be at the surgery center at 6:15 a.m., so I wasn't awake enough to be too scared. I've been dreading this for weeks—not the surgery as much as the after care. It's scary doing something like this when you're living alone. I remember how much care I gave Bill after his surgery. Now it's just me.

I arranged with Robin to pick me up after the surgery, and the surgeon's orders were for me to have twenty-four hours in care at my house, so I asked David and Sharon. Thank goodness they had no plans.

But things changed quickly. I don't have any memory of this, but after surgery my vitals and my oxygen levels weren't staying steady. I guess I was awake during this time, but I don't remember any of it. After hours of waiting, the surgeon decided to have me transferred to nearby West Allis hospital. I don't remember any of that either. I was admitted and stayed for two nights.

Saturday, April 26, 2014

This morning I guess I was looking better, so I came home this afternoon—with no memory of what happened since 6:15 a.m. last Thursday. I do have a vague memory of eating Chinese food for dinner with David and Sharon, but that's it. I was told they gave me two doses of my medication prescribed by the surgeon, probably one in the evening and one in the morning, but I also don't remember this.

Sunday, April 27, 2014

David and Sharon tell me that we had breakfast together, which I don't remember. I was very tired this morning, so it was decided that I should stay home while they went to church. Roger was to come over later.

Fr. Pat and Robin decided to come to my house after church. They found me unconscious with my lips blue, and called Roger. Roger came over right away, driving his car right up to my front door. He lifted me up and put me in his car. I was told I was doing quite a bit of screaming—most likely because of my shoulder. He took me back to West Allis, where the admission diagnosis was hypoxia (the body is deprived of oxygen).

My ordeal in the emergency room was horrible. I only remember my part in it—I was screaming in pain, and I kept yelling at them to let me die. I'm sure the staff was working hard... changing my clothes, trying to keep me in one place, and adding needles to my left arm for my vitals. I was probably doing the worst to myself by moving my right arm incoherently. I vaguely remember them taking me to the ICU.

Monday, April 28, 2014

A 24/7 team of nursing assistants was assigned to me. They were to stay in my room at all times. For a couple of days they had to help me use bedpans and get anything I needed. In other words, I wasn't to move anywhere. My confusion was mixing with reality, making the staff seem more like jailers to me. I also seemed to feel that when I was better, they might be putting me into inpatient therapy. I was starting to think they might take away my house and Lady—I was petrified. I tried to keep as quiet as possible, and I was trying to look as mentally capable as possible, but this was difficult since my memory was going in and out—more often out.

Tuesday, April 29, 2014

Today was a day of total confusion for me. Most of the day I was hallucinating that my nursing assistant on call was pushing my bed all over the hospital. I feared the nurses; I was afraid they would suggest I go into a residency home or rehab facility. I was still scared they would take my home and my dog away from me. Even though some of the nurses were friendly, they felt like my jailers. And then there were a couple of nursing assistants who treated me in a condescending manner.

Wednesday, April 30, 2014

Although I began having moments of clearer thinking, I would fall asleep and be surprised that things and people had changed. A couple of times I awoke to find myself face to face with someone who was talking to me. I couldn't figure out why they hadn't seen that I was sleeping. I drifted on and off rather often.

When Roger and Beth came by to visit in the evening, things became more real to me. But I still thought all of my strange hallucinations were true, and I told Roger about the horrible things that were happening. He gently reminded me that I was having trouble remembering things right now; that stopped me while I thought about what he said. But it still didn't make sense to me.

Thursday, May 1, 2014

Finally, I awoke thinking much more clearly. And I finally was allowed to use the bathroom with assistance. Thank goodness, no more bedpans. I also was allowed to clean up at the sink in my room. It was quite awkward since I had my arm in a sling from the rotator cuff surgery, and it was quite uncomfortable, mostly because there was a strap that went across my body. The material was like wool. It always felt warm and it always seemed to be edging up near my neck. It left me feeling claustrophobic quite a bit of the time.

When the medical doctor came in to check me out, I told him I would like to be discharged soon. He said I was admitted under a psychiatrist, so she would have to see me and decide when I would be discharged. I wasn't very pleased, since this psychiatrist hadn't come to see me all these days. Of course she may have when I was really out of it—but we hadn't had a talk since I was coming back to my senses. I hoped the medical doctor would talk with the psychiatrist for me.

That afternoon I was sent to rehab to start a few simple movements for my arm, and to regain my leg movements. I was told that for every day you lay in bed, your legs get stiffer and weaker. I felt a little stiff, but I was feeling better as the day went on. But I still was having some disorientation.

One of the surgeons saw me and pulled some of the bandages off my shoulder to see how it was doing. He seemed pleased with my recovery. It did hurt when he was doing it, so my thoughts were that he had just pulled a bunch of skin from my shoulder. Later I realized what he had done, but I was shaken at the time. Luckily I didn't say anything.

Late in the afternoon, while I was still in rehab, someone took my blood pressure and found that it was 195/85. That wasn't normal for me, and the physical therapist didn't look very happy. She wanted to put another needle in my left arm to get a better lead. I had a lot of needles in my arm, but they were taped down because the veins had dried up. It was quite disconcerting knowing my veins weren't flowing very well.

She tried a couple of times to get a new line started, but with no success. Then they called a service with expert phlebotomists. It took about half an hour, but one finally showed up. He tried three times with no success. Now I was getting very nervous. They kept telling me to relax, but lying on my back, one arm in a sling; the other severely punctured by so many near misses, and feeling very warm, wasn't calming me down. But I was trying to breathe slowing and consistently.

There was a lot of talking going on amongst staff, until finally another nurse came in to take her turn with it. I recognized her as one of the lead nurses, so my hopes were high. She sat down and began her search; as she felt around, I could tell she was getting her needle ready, and pop, she had it in. I felt such relief and thanked her immensely. They were finally able to give me some sort of blood pressure medicine to try to lower my BP.

By then I was exhausted, and fortunately I was able to go back to my room. The uncomfortable part of going to sleep was that I had to lie on my back with both of my arms straight. Since I couldn't sleep on my back, that made it difficult to get any rest. I would sleep for about an hour and then wake up and have to go to the bathroom, which meant waking up the nursing assistant who had to walk to the bathroom with me and wait until I was finished.

Friday, May 2, 2014

I awoke to the news that there was a nursing student who would be my aide today. She was very friendly and upbeat, just what I needed. She helped me clean up and wash my hair.

It was so much easier with her helping. Since my BP was still in question, she was carefully making sure she captured the numbers correctly. Thank goodness she decided to check my BP on my leg; apparently my arm looked too beat up. It was still 195/85, which caused some concern, so they were going to check it periodically during the day.

Later on, after a couple more checks, my BP lowered to around 154/85—still high for me, but much better. Everything seemed to be improving. And I had quite a surprise. The nursing assistant that took care of me the first few days came in to see me. She was very friendly and soft-spoken. And I had been so mean to her, at times shouting for help and trying to kick her to get away. I smiled at her and apologized for being so mean. She said not to worry about it and that it happens all the time. That was so sad.

Finally, the psychiatrist came into my room. She had steely eyes and tight lips—no smiles here. She asked me a couple of questions, and then I let her know I would like to go home. Her cold response was, "How do I know you won't try to kill yourself again?"

I wanted to get into it with her—insisting that I hadn't tried to kill myself that somehow the mixture of the pills I was on and the surgery meds must not have mixed well. But I stopped myself and said nothing. I knew I had no chance of changing her mind.

She walked out without a goodbye or an "I'll see you tomorrow." Nothing. That was it.

That evening, I spent a lot of time thinking about how many patients in the hospital were scared or confused or felt they were alone and powerless. It made me really sad to think of them, especially since I had just experienced it. I said a prayer for all of them.

The medical doctor was early today. He checked me out, asked me a couple of questions, and then smiled and said I was to be discharged today. I was thrilled. I didn't want to call Roger because it was too early for him, so I called Tommy to see if he could pick me up. I remembered to ask him to bring me some clothes. I never saw my clothes in the room, so I figured they got cut up in the ER.

The nurse wrote out my discharge papers and went through them with me. I laughed (secretly) when she showed me my discharge med instructions. I had been off all psych meds since I was admitted, but on the discharge papers it said to take all my previous medications. If I did that, I'd probably be back here in the morning. I decided to call Dr. John to ask him what I should take.

Tommy showed up, and I got dressed. He had picked out clothes that were a little tight on me, so it took me forever to take off the sling, pull the sweatshirt on, and put the sling back on. *But I did it!* I told myself. *I'm going home. This nightmare is almost over.*

Tommy was very attentive getting me home and settled. It all felt wonderful, except for Lady still being at Roger's house. I waited before calling him, because I knew he would want me to stay at his house for a while. It would be nice to have Roger and Terry taking care of me, but I sure was anticipating sleeping in my own bed.

Finally, I called Roger. He was surprised they had let me go so early in the morning and disappointed because he had wanted to talk with the doctor or nurses about my aftercare. I told him Tommy had to leave soon, but that was okay; Roger said he'd be over to get me in a little while. Of course with Roger, that meant in a few hours. That was fine for me, because I wanted to change clothes again and go through some of my mail.

I thanked Tommy and went about my chores until Roger showed up to get me. I was eager to see Lady, and once we arrived at Roger's house, I hugged her tight. Of course Roger's dogs, Serena and Mela, wanted attention too; so did the cats. I was down to one arm, but I felt I needed about six of them. I sat down and ignored all of them so I could relax my arm. I was also quite tired, so I was ready to relax all of me.

Terry made a wonderful dinner, and soon I was stretched out on the couch, ready to get some sleep.

Sunday, May 4, through Wednesday, May 7, 2014

Over the next few days I got a lot of rest at Roger and Terry's house. Terry cooked some great meals, and I enjoyed their company. Dr. John called Roger on Monday to see how I was doing. I answered Roger's phone and was surprised to hear Dr. John's voice. I told him what the hospital discharge papers said about resuming all of my medications and how that didn't sound right to me. Dr. John agreed and told me to restart only one of my meds. He would see me on Thursday.

Roger drove Lady and me home on Wednesday night. After that, Tommy would become my driver for some time, until my shoulder healed.

Thursday, May 8, 2014

Tommy drove me to my appointment with Dr. John. I told Dr. John how horrible all of this had been for me— especially the first few days at the West Allis hospital. Then we discussed the medications. He said he wants to take it slow with my meds to see how I'm doing. I complained that I felt the surgeon and his staff hadn't properly checked on what I was taking for meds, and I felt this had caused a lot of my problems. And when the hospital took me off all meds, I had a few days of severe withdrawal, which caused my memory loss and confusion.

Dr. John listened to my complaints. Even though he said little, I felt he might be agreeing with some of them.

I asked Dr. John if I could also have my pill to help me sleep; he agreed to one at bedtime. That was less than before, but I'd agree to anything right now.

Friday, May 9, 2014

I saw Ken today. It had been quite a long time since my last session with him. I gave him a recap of the last couple of weeks and the problems with my medications. I told him I agreed with Dr. John on starting me back slow, but I was worried about my anxiety. He said we'd have to see what Dr. John did in the next couple of weeks.

Saturday, May 10, and Sunday, May 11, 2014

The rest of the weekend I was alone. My anxiety was pretty bad, and I felt panicky. I mostly stayed in my lounge chair and tried to find something on TV to help me forget— forget everything I've just been through.

Monday, May 12, 2014

Today was my follow-up appointment with the surgeon. I was shocked because the first thing he asked me was whether I needed a refill of my pain meds. I asked him if he knew what had happened to me after the surgery—referring to my week-long hospital stay. But he responded as if he were just talking about the problem I'd had right after the surgery with my vitals and oxygen levels.

Could it be that he wasn't aware I'd been in the hospital all week? Wow! It wasn't worth bringing up, though. I told him I didn't need a refill of the strong meds, but asked if I could have a prescription for Tylenol 3. He said yes, and then set me up to start rehab this week. I would start tomorrow and go twice a week. I was glad about that—I knew I needed guidance to start my rehab.

Tuesday, May 13, 2014

I was scheduled for about six weeks of rehab with Megan. She was great—she started slow, and I was glad because it didn't hurt very much. She also gave me exercises to do at home. When I asked about starting to use the arm machine that had been delivered to my home, she was surprised I hadn't been using it yet. But once I told her my story of going to the hospital and then to my brother's house, she understood. She said to start using it right away.

Wednesday, May 14, 2014

During my appointment with Dr. John today, he asked how I'm doing—as usual. I told him I'm doing terrible. My anxiety just keeps bothering me, and I can't stand it anymore. He started me on a new medication to help with this. I have my fingers crossed.

Friday, May 16, 2014

Ken asked me at our appointment today if Dr. John had added anything to my medications. I explained he added a new med that seemed to decrease my anxiety a little, but not enough. I can still feel it, and it makes me feel like drinking again. Ken reminded me to talk with Dr. John on Wednesday, and I told him that's my plan.

Saturday, May 17, and Sunday, May 18, 2014

Once again, the rest of the weekend was lonely. I continued to notice how much anxiety I was still feeling. I was pleasantly surprised that my arm didn't hurt too much. I didn't even need to use the Tylenol 3. I'd take one before each therapy appointment.

Monday, May 19, 2014

I didn't have any plans or appointments, and Tommy couldn't work today. So I'm still alone and anxious. Not a good combination.

Tuesday, May 20, 2014

I had my appointment with Diana in the morning and Megan (my physical therapist) in the afternoon. That was good—I needed some direction to my day.

Diana and I talked about her medication debate. Her viewpoint was to use no medications. I didn't agree with that, because I remembered how I felt before starting them. I felt like I was going crazy, and I was only sleeping a couple of hours a night. My anxiety was horrible. I cried all the time. I guess you don't always agree with your therapist.

In my session with Megan, I quickly learned that if I did one exercise last week, I'd be doing two this week. A little more pain, but not too bad—I was up for the challenge. I wanted full use of my arm again.

Wednesday, May 21, 2014

When I walked into Dr. John's office today, I was ready with my questions. As usual, he started off our session with a couple of questions about how I was doing. This week, the answer was, "Terrible." My overwhelming anxiety was driving me crazy. I felt panicky, trapped. He asked if I had any dizziness or confusion on the medications I was on now; I told him no. He said I seemed clear-minded. He decided to double the times of day that I was taking my current anti- anxiety med. At least that was something.

Friday, May 23, 2014

Another session with Ken this morning; he also asked how I was doing with the meds Dr. John prescribed. I said I still had anxiety, but I told him Dr. John had just increased the dosage from one anti-anxiety pill to two. I hoped it would help.

And in the afternoon, I had a physical therapy session with Megan. Those are going well. My arm is getting stronger and more mobile every session.

Saturday, May 24, 2014

I was filled with tension today, unable to concentrate on much of anything. Once again, I relied on the TV. What is building in me now is a feeling of dread, due to the closeness of the anniversary of the day we met: May 28th. I don't want to go through another of these anniversaries without Bill.

Sunday, May 25, 2014

I finally made it to church, the first time since my surgery. Denzel and Brenda picked me up on their way to church. It was difficult saying hi to everyone after such a gap in my attendance had taken place. I felt quite tearful, but I tried very hard to hold it in.

The rest of my day, I was filled with sad thoughts of Bill—although for a few minutes I had happy thoughts of when we met, which then made me cry.

I need to have another talk with Dr. John. I know this is going to get worse.

Monday, May 26, 2014

Today was Memorial Day. Roger called me and asked me if he could pick me up to take me to his house for dinner. At first I didn't want to, but I said okay anyway.

That turned out to be a good choice. I'd spent too much alone time, and it was a good break to go to Roger and Terry's house. Terry made a delicious dinner, and I had fun watching all the pets running around.

In talking with Roger, I reminded him that the anniversary of our first meeting was coming up this Wednesday, and it was getting me down. I stayed for a while   longer, and then Roger drove me home.

Tuesday, May 27, 2014

I had one appointment today—with Megan. She noticed I looked down, so I told her about the anniversary tomorrow. I was lucky to get Megan for my physical therapy. She's such a nice girl. She talked with me for a while about it, wanting to make sure I'll be okay.

Back at home, my tension kept increasing; I couldn't stop thinking about tomorrow.

Wednesday, May 28, 2014

The anniversary of the first time Bill and I met. When I awoke, I was already crying. Lying in bed was always difficult, but with an anniversary it was torture. I caught myself drifting in thought a couple of times, but then I decided to get out of bed. It wasn't helping to just lie there.

I usually love Wednesday morning Bible study, but I was afraid I might get too emotional this morning. But I had no choice, since the group would be on their way soon. I ended up getting a lot of hugs when they arrived. Fr. Pat isn't much of a hugger, but he gave me a nice hug today; that helped. I had sorely missed all the hugs Bill used to give me, so I took them all in, with a few sniffles and teary eyes. But I got through it.

In the afternoon I had my weekly appointment with Dr. John. I started to cry as soon as I sat down in his office. I tried to explain how the past week had gone, and I told him about today's special meaning. He was very sympathetic and tried talking with me for a while, saying how hard this must be for me. He said this with such sincerity that I knew he truly tried to understand.

We then discussed my anxiety again; I told him it was still horrible. This time, after asking if I felt clear-headed, he agreed to put me back on one of my other anti-anxiety meds. I was grateful because I knew that would help me, especially through this evening.

Back at home, I knew it was time to just think about Bill and me. The attraction we had felt the night we first met was obvious. The good conversation we had was remarkable. The feelings in our hearts were unmistakable.

I went through quite a few tissues tonight.

Early June 2014

My days are filled with appointments: my shoulder surgeon, Diana, Megan, my Bible study, Dr. John, my DPT therapy group, my second Bible study, and Ken. And in between these appointments, I'm supposed to exercise my shoulder every day. It doesn't leave much time open for anything else. But toward mid-June I knew what was coming closer—the anniversary of Bill's accident. The tension inside me was already mounting.

Wednesday, June 18, 2014

I would have preferred to have this day to myself to think about Bill, but first I had Bible study. It was probably a good thing because I could focus on something religious, which was the point of my thoughts. Unfortunately, I was feeling quite anxious and nervous, so I hoped I'd be able to concentrate.

And next, I had my appointment with Dr. John. That also was a good thing. We talked about the anniversary and my emotions. I cried as usual, but the session helped.

I think of this date as the last day I saw Bill before his accident. We had such a wonderful evening, riding our motorcycle, having dinner at a nearby restaurant, playing with the dogs, and getting to bed early. But then the rainstorm— that terrible rainstorm that brought about everything else. It also brought about a nervousness in me that was stronger than usual.

Thursday, June 19, 2014

On that fateful night, it was 1:00 a.m. by the time we were starting to fall asleep. Everything seemed fine—until the phone rang. The rain had caused flooding downtown, and Bill was being asked to come back to work. I felt sick. I was worried and afraid.

Those two days were difficult for me to relive. I did a lot of praying—that Bill was in Heaven, and that I would somehow live through this loneliness. That I would follow God's will, not my own. That I would someday go to Heaven to meet Jesus, and that he would take me to Bill.

Monday, June 22, 2014

This week a few of my appointments were cancelled, so I snuck in seeing some of my friends. Monday I saw Robin and Helene at Helene's house for dinner. She had just moved, so I hadn't seen her house yet. It was beautiful, and she had furnished it wonderfully. We had a pleasant dinner on her patio, with all of us talking up a storm.

I knew Helene from our last church, St. Edmund's. She hadn't come along on our vagabond trip to find another church, so it was great to see her again. And I was glad for her to meet Fr. Pat's wife, Robin. Secretly I was trying to get Helene to rejoin us, and it's looking hopeful.

Thursday, June 26, 2014

Today I met Rosemary for coffee (tea, for her). We tried to meet every couple of weeks just to talk. Our conversations were always a great pleasure for me. We would mix our small talk and catching up with talk of the Father, the Son, and the Holy Spirit. I was learning so much from Rosemary, and along with my Bible study, my increased knowledge of the Bible was heartwarming. It gave me hope. And I wanted to learn more.

Saturday, June 28, 2014

Today Beth's daughters are holding a surprise sixtieth birthday party for their mom. It was worth going just to laugh at Beth getting older. Beth is five months older than I am, and since we were kids I have always rubbed it in. I didn't pick on her today, though, because it was actually a month before the big day. The kids knew the only way to surprise her was having it so early. I heard Beth telling people again and again that she isn't sixty yet!

Monday, June 30, 2014

This week my appointment with Dr. John was on a Monday. He knew I was having a rough time of it, as this was the time of year Bill had been in the hospital and we were all so desperately worried about him. I dropped into a deep depression and didn't want to leave my house except for my appointments. But I did keep busy with those appointments.

Tuesday, July 1, 2014

I had to see Megan and Diana today. I was also remembering the anniversary of Mom's death. This time of year held too much heartache for me. Mom and I had been so close. After my dad died, she lived with Bill and me for around fifteen years. I still have moments when I have vivid memories of her.

Wednesday, July 2, 2014

Luckily there was no Bible study this week. That made it easier on me. But I did have an appointment with my primary doctor.

Thursday, July 3, 2014

Today I had to see Megan and Ken.

I felt distressed this evening because I knew of the big celebration of fireworks at the lakefront. Bill and I used to enjoy that a lot, which means that I didn't want to think about it. It was a cool night, so I closed my windows. Unfortunately I still heard them. I thought of the fun we used to have, taking the motorcycle down to the lakefront at the last minute, but still being able to park between a couple of cars and walk to the bridge where we could see them clearly.

Friday, July 4, 2014 — Fourth of July

This holiday doesn't exist for me anymore. Too much sadness. My memories are of me in Bill's hospital room, praying for him, and looking out the little window at the lake and the boats traveling around waiting for the fireworks.

Again, it was cool tonight, so I closed my windows and spent a very lonely night. We used to have such fun on this day that it was hard to even think about it. I kept the TV on loud so I wouldn't hear the fireworks. When they were over, I went to bed in tears.

Saturday, July 5, 2014

A quiet day at home, feeling the sadness of the next day. The unbelievable day that took my husband away from me. Just when we thought he was getting a little bit better.

Sunday, July 6, 2014

The anniversary of Bill's death. The worst day of my life. My love, my partner, gone.

I want to join him. I want to be in Heaven.

Mid July 2014

The majority of the month was filled with appointments and sessions with Diana, Meagan, Dr. John, Ken, and the DPT group, along with Bible study. I didn't want to see anyone else.

Sunday, July 20, 2014

Today is Will's first real birthday party. He will be two years old on July 25th. It was nice to get the family together again for this celebration. Many more!

Wednesday, July 23, 2014

I saw Dr. John today, and I was quite upset during my session. I explained that I had been having more difficulty since the last (fifth) anniversary of Bill's death. He reminded me to use our "contract" if I needed it. That meant I should call him or the hospital if I were in need.

Thursday, July 24, 2014

I had my DPT group meeting today with Diana. I mostly just sat and kept quiet. I just didn't feel like talking.

Friday, July 25, 2014

In my session with Ken today, I was quite excitable… crying and carrying on about how much I want to die. Ken wanted to walk me to the intake office of the psych hospital, but I told him I finally had plans to go to my brother's house. He said okay to that, but after that, he recommended that I should think about what I should do next. He thought it was still a good idea to admit myself on Saturday or Sunday.

I let Roger know I was thinking about going into the hospital. He looked sad, but agreed that might be the best.

Saturday, July 26, 2014

Beth and I met to do a little rummaging, run a couple of errands, and have lunch—and best of all, Beth talked me into having a pedicure with her. I was nervous, but it felt so good that I definitely want to have another one sometime.

I decided to tell her during lunch that I'm thinking about going into the hospital. It's something I get nervous about telling her because she usually gets upset. As I told Beth, she said it might be a good thing to do, but then she appeared to be angry; she told me I only think of myself, and then, that I don't think of her before myself and others.

I was saddened to hear her say these things, but I just sat and listened to her. I didn't agree with her, but I knew that arguing about it wasn't going to make a difference. I wish Beth realized how important she is to me. But I don't want her worrying about me all the time, so I put off telling her some things.

This evening I felt heartsick, and I prayed to God, asking him if I could go to Heaven now. I decided to go into the hospital tomorrow (Sunday), but I don't feel like going to church tomorrow because I don't feel like talking with anyone.

Sunday, July 27, 2014—
Inpatient hospitalization (16 days)

I got things ready to go to the hospital and called a few people to let them know where I was going. Tommy's fiancée, Melissa, was going to pick me and Lady up, and drop Lady off at Roger's house before taking me to the hospital.

Once I said goodbye to Melissa, I headed to the intake area and realized I had forgotten my purse. I felt panicked, but thank goodness they were still able to register me without my insurance cards. Of course, I was in their records. Then I realized my address book, which had everyone's phone numbers in it, and my calendar that showed my schedule were also in my purse—I could cry. Now everything was going to be difficult. And then, worse news: Dr. John was on vacation, not returning till Tuesday. My heart sagged, and my anxiety rose. Now I would need another doctor until Dr. John was back. I hated that.

It took a couple of hours to finish the registration process, and then I was ready to go into the unit. I walked down the hall with a staff person, hoping we would be heading toward Unit 3. I had been in both Unit 3 and Unit 4 and much preferred Unit 3 for the staff and the size of the unit. We turned the corner to go to Unit 4. Ugh. But oh well, nothing to do about it now.

I was escorted to the front desk, and two nursing assistants walked with me to my room. I had brought very little this time, so there wasn't much to search through. And with no purse, that saved a lot of time. I was also pleasantly surprised that they had toned down the body search. It was quicker and not so embarrassing.

By the time they finally left me alone in my room, it was 10:30 p.m. I was grateful to be exhausted, because I would be seeing a new doctor in the morning, and that always made me nervous. The stress of coming here always made me tired anyway. I fell asleep quite quickly and slept the entire night.

Monday, July 28, 2014

After breakfast this morning, I still felt exhausted, so I went back to bed until lunchtime. I knew I wasn't allowed to go to the group meetings until I saw a doctor, and he hadn't come yet, so I figured I might as well sleep. And I needed it badly. I had endured a lot of activity yesterday and, with the weakness from my shoulder injury, I could probably sleep the day away. And that didn't even take into account my anxiety and depression. Those wore me out too.

In the afternoon I had a chance to talk with my therapist; she seemed decent. Next a physician's assistant came to give me a medical check-up. At least I had some company for a little while—the hours were passing so slowly.

After dinner, I was glad that I had brought my Bible; I started reading it, and that helped me feel a little better. The problem I had with the Bible was keeping my concentration going. At times I was fine, but with everything else, my thoughts of Bill always crept in. Maybe Bill was trying to tell me something, like, "Jean, concentrate on the Bible."

The psychiatrist finally came to see me at 8:00 p.m. I felt sorry for him, having to work so late. I was told he does his rounds quite late, but 8:00 p.m.? He seemed nice, and he moved fast. That actually seemed to be helping me stay more awake and sharper, thinking I needed to stay at the same pace to keep up.

He did a thorough examination of my story, my thoughts, and my actions. But his being nice didn't keep him from being direct with me. He asked me detailed questions about how I had been affected by Bill's death—the heartache and loneliness. He asked about my suicide thoughts and plans. He wanted me to thoroughly explain them to him to try to keep me safe.

I tried to follow his instructions. I told him that I liked him fine, but that I wanted my regular psychiatrist, Dr. John, because I had been seeing him for five years and he knew me well. Dr. Michael said he would call Dr. John and fill him in; I was relieved. He decided to change my medications some, adding one and changing another. I was curious about what Dr. John would think.

When our session finally ended, I was very tired and knew I'd be going to bed right away. But I had probably had too many naps—I was very fidgety, and I did a lot of moving around and listening to noises coming from the unit.

Tuesday, July 29, 2014

Now that I had seen a psychiatrist, I could go to the group sessions today. I wasn't always crazy about them, but at least they were a distraction, and sometimes a good one. I was very tense most of the time, so anything to relax me was good. And at times something really poignant came up and everyone in the group would become one as they listened to the person speaking. And sometimes, the person speaking was me.

I kept watching for Dr. John. His absence was increasing my anxiety, since I wasn't sure if he'd be coming today. Finally Dr. Michael appeared, saying I'd be seeing him. I didn't mind him, but I was hurt Dr. John hadn't shown up, and my unhappiness grew.

Reading my Bible was good, for a while. Tonight we got to watch a movie; that was a nice change of pace. I was missing my TV at home, especially as a distraction. By the time the movie was done, I was ready for bed.

Tonight I didn't sleep very well; I woke up with gurgling in my stomach, like I might throw up. I spent the next hour sitting up in bed. The checker (the staff person who comes in every fifteen minutes to see if you're okay) asked if I'd like to see the nurse for something to settle my stomach. I agreed and headed to the nurses' station. She gave me something, and I went back to sitting up in bed.

A couple of hours later, the checker again asked if I was okay. Apparently I had fallen asleep sitting up, so I told her I was okay and lay down. I was out after that, and I think I pretty much slept most of the rest of the night.

Wednesday, July 30, 2014

I woke up Wednesday, hoping to see Dr. John early today. During breakfast, Dr. Michael stopped in and told me Dr. John would be seeing me today. I thanked him, and I was thrilled. My anxiety lessened a little, knowing things would be getting more routine. But next I had to go to the group session.

Today we were to look through colorful magazines and photocopied quotes from the Bible. Then we were to make a picture out of them. What at first seemed like a silly assignment became quite interesting, and my picture came out quite nice.

When I returned to my room, a nurse's assistant told me Dr. John was here to see me. Yes! I was still upset that he hadn't seen me yesterday, so of course I had to bring it up. He said he didn't know until yesterday afternoon that I'd been admitted. I felt a bit foolish for asking and immediately dropped the subject.

He asked how I was doing and what was going on. I explained I had continued to be anxious and depressed, and I was having thoughts of suicide again. I told him that Dr. Michael had changed some of my meds; Dr. John looked at them and told me he would check. He reminded me he'd see me tomorrow. That evening, I found out Dr. John had increased my dosage of those meds, so I felt better.

Another woman, named Denise, had been admitted on Monday. I tried to talk with her a couple of times, but I was told she had overdosed, and she was still quite out of it. She spent most of her days and nights crying (almost screaming). The nurses were trying to quiet her down, somewhat for our sake, but it wasn't helping. She sounded so sad that I didn't mind the noise.

I said hello to her and had lunch at her table in the cafeteria, and I decided I should try to talk with her more often. I quickly noticed that she was enjoying my companionship. When I would be going to someplace like group or lunch, I started asking her if she was going also. She nearly always smiled, seeming pleased, and walked along with me. She slowly started to talk a little more and cry less—and she was good company for me, as well.

By today she had almost completely stopped crying, and she was looking much better. She told me she hadn't overdosed on purpose. At home, she had still felt upset, so she had taken one more pill. It reminded me how easily that could happen.

This evening, our recreation was Wii bowling, a type of interactive video game, and when I told her I was going to play, she also agreed to join in. It was a fun game and a good change of pace. And I was so pleased that I could help her a little.

At bedtime tonight, the same thing happened as I went to bed—I had stomach problems again. This was frustrating. I went back to the nurses' station, and she gave me the same thing as last night. I went back to bed, sitting up in the corner of my bed again. Eventually I slid down and got some sleep.

Thursday, July 31, 2014

I awoke to the call for breakfast. This was the first morning I heard that familiar sound because the intercom system hadn't been working very well until today. I got up because I also wanted to get ready in case Dr. John came early. I ate, had my vitals checked, and came back to my room.

I did some reading until my 9:30 a.m. group session began. It was a quiet group due to a rather large pile of handouts for us to read. There also was an outdoor walk available in the garden, which didn't much interest me because it was warm and muggy. I thought maybe I'd take a walk later.

I went back to my room to read, and then Dr. John arrived. Of course he asked how I was doing. My reply was, "Not so well." I was experiencing the full package of sadness, anxiety, depression, and thoughts of suicide. He looked concerned and started asking me questions about what may have started all this. He said he knew how hard the summer was for me. The anniversaries, the events that I missed. I told him I wasn't shaking these feelings; in fact, they were getting worse. And the worse they were, the more isolated I wanted to be. Then our session time was up, and he said he'd see me tomorrow.

I rested a while, wanting time to think about what he said. It was soon lunchtime, so I headed to where the trays were. I joined Denise in the cafeteria. We were becoming a pair. Now that she was feeling better, it was nice to talk with her. She would still get nervous, but she was having fewer panic attacks and was crying much less. In fact, I told her I was crying more than she was, so she had to help me now. I started to join her for walks down the hallway. At the end of the hallway were two seats, where we would sit and talk for a while, and then walk back—two Olympic sprinters!

There was only one afternoon session because one of the therapists was out sick. Instead, they were having a longer outdoor garden walk. I was already feeling melancholy, so I chose not to walk, but to stay inside and write my notes.

After that, the patients and staff decided to play Wii bowling again. I joined in and amazingly, I beat the three other participants, including two men who were regular bowlers. I finished with a score of 167, which was a shocker, as I am a lousy bowler in real life.

Done with that excitement, I decided to go to bed. Once again, after resting for a while, my stomach was upset. Back to the nurses' station for a pill again. But this time I fell asleep after a short while.

Friday, August 1, 2014

The breakfast call woke me up again, which was good because I had been sound asleep. Denise and I had breakfast together—the last time, because she was being discharged today. I started wondering when I would be discharged. Today seemed too soon, but you never really know until the doctor tells you.

The morning group session began. The therapist had an example of an "I Am" poem. I thought it would be silly, but it wasn't. Below is my version:

I am loving and kind
I wonder when I will see my husband again
I hear his voice
I see his face
I want to be with him
I am loving and kind
I pretend I am in his arms
I feel his touch
I touch him back
I worry about my lack of patience
I cry when I miss him
I am in his arms
I understand I will join him someday
I have deep faith in God
I dream about Heaven
I try to wait my turn.
I hope that day will come soon
I am hopeful that I will join him someday.

I felt teary-eyed after writing my poem during that session, and I asked my nurse on duty if we could talk. I told him how sad, depressed, anxious, and suicidal I'm feeling. He suggested that I find new interests, find a new life… all those things I don't want to do. I felt more upset after talking with him, but that wasn't his fault.

Dr. John soon arrived, and we had a good session. I explained all of the symptoms to him that I had just shared with my nurse, letting him know they were still bothering me. He started asking me questions about my thoughts of suicide. Did I have a plan?

I told him I always have a plan. I had one as soon as I got into my room on Sunday night. He asked me what the plan was.

I suddenly felt embarrassed to have to explain it—but I did. I would use my clothing to hang myself from the bathroom door.

The room got quiet. A couple more things were said, and then Dr. John said I wouldn't be going home tonight. I agreed.

He left, and I had my lunch with Denise. We went for a short walk and sat at the end of the hallway, but then my unit therapist wanted to talk with me. We talked for a while, and she showed me a safety plan she was completing for me. It had to do with activities I should try. It also listed numbers I should call if I had a crisis, or checking into the hospital—if yes, again. I had to sign it, and a copy went into my file.

It was time for another walk in the garden; this time I decided to go. I walked halfway this time—very impressive. But again, it felt quite warm out, so I went back inside. Another walk with Denise, and then back to my room to read.

Denise's husband arrived to take her home. I knew I would miss her, but we did exchange phone numbers. One last hug and she was gone. I didn't feel like participating in any activities, so I decided to stay in my room and write notes. Or so I thought.

I felt restless, so I went into the movie room, where someone else was watching a movie. After a good conversation instead of seeing the movie, I noticed that a woman had come into the unit to be admitted.

She came in loudly, touching everyone and being overly friendly. And as fast as flipping a switch, she turned into a pushy, bad-mouthed woman, walking into her room and tearing pictures off the walls, yelling, and ordering me into her room. Needless to say, I didn't go, although she continued to yell at me.

Finally, two building guards responded, and the woman punched one of them in the face. They put the woman into a "quiet" room next to the nurses' station. The room has a stretcher bed with straps to hold the patient quiet. They gave her meds to slow her down, and then they were going to put her in her room after she was asleep.

That wasn't good enough for me; I was the only other female down that hallway, and I knew I'd be afraid to sleep in case she came into my room. So I requested I either be moved to the male side down the other hallway, or, preferably, be moved to Unit 3. They chose to have me move to the male side, so I had to pick up my stuff and take it to the new room. But I still didn't feel safe—my anxiety was all over the place. I chose to leave the light on.

A nurse came to check on me later. She was very nice, and she talked with me for quite a while, trying to calm me down and telling me how brave I was. I didn't feel very brave, but it was nice to hear. Eventually I fell asleep.

Saturday, August 2, 2014

I awoke to a nursing assistant telling me breakfast was here. I must have slept right through the announcement. I didn't feel like eating, but I thought I better have something in case Dr. John came for rounds. I only ate a little; then I had my vitals taken. My blood pressure was at 150/85, which was quite high for me—but no surprise after last night's activities. I got my meds, and the nurse saw that I was agitated. I went back to my room and lay down again.

I had drifted off when Dr. John tapped on my door and came in. He saw that I was upset, and I told him about last night and the woman who had frightened me. I explained that I was extremely nervous, but a lot of it had started before the woman arrived. My anxiety rose when she started yelling at me, and I still felt shaky this morning. He reminded me he'd be seeing me on Monday, but that felt like a long time in the future while I sat here scared.

The new woman was still locked up, thank goodness.

They were still missing a therapist today, so we didn't meet until 3 p.m. I called Robin to let her know I won't be at church tomorrow. And I called Helena, who told me she's stopping by in a few minutes. Time for a break.

What a very special visit with Helena. She came with three packets of flowers—yellow mums and zinnias, and a small purple flower similar to a daisy. They are so nice to look at. We conversed about our last couple of weeks, and then Helena read to me from her Bible before leaving.

And then I couldn't believe it—in walked David and Sharon holding a plate of caramel chocolate brownies. The brownies were more than delicious. We then played a few hands of Uno. I was defeated by those pros, and then it was their time to leave.

I decided to call Roger, and he said he was coming for a visit. How nice! A while later, Roger arrived with a much-wanted soda and candy bar. I could have gained ten pounds tonight, but I controlled myself. Roger was good company; everyone was good company tonight.

I told Roger how the week was going and about the crazy lady Friday night. She had scared me, and I wasn't very comfortable with what they were going to do with her. But Roger had helped me relax; it was a good visit.

By the time he left, I was tired. I got my meds and was delighted to see a couple of the prescriptions had been increased. *Thank you, Dr. John,* I thought. I climbed into bed, but soon found out I had indigestion again. So I got up to see the nurse again, and then went back to my room. I was soon asleep.

I awoke to a tap on my door for breakfast. I couldn't figure out if the loudspeaker was out again or if I was sleeping through it, but I went to the dining room and picked up my yogurt and cranberry juice. My stomach was still in a knot. As I ate my breakfast, the psychotic woman came into the cafeteria to try to talk with a couple of people. I couldn't believe she was allowed in the dining area with us.

When I left to get my vitals and pills, the troublesome woman was at the nurses' desk, near where I was standing. I left to go back to my room, and I took a shower. By the time I was done, it was time for the first group meeting of the day. After talking for a while, we left for our break before our next session.

I lay down, planning to rest for fifteen minutes, but soon fell asleep for a solid hour and missed the second session altogether. So I decided to read in my chair in my room. I had been there for a while when there was a knock on my door. I said hello, and the psychotic woman came through the door, closing it behind her.

I was so scared—I wasn't sure what to do. She came toward me and was whispering and slurring her words, so it was hard to understand anything she said. It was something about her and a group of people who "were going to be leaving" (the hospital, I guessed), so I knew she was fantasizing.

She told me I couldn't use my bathroom or shower, which made no sense to me. Then she noticed my reading glasses and said she wanted them. I handed them over to her—they were from the nurses' station anyway, and I didn't want to make her angry. I stood up, trying to think of a way I could get out of my room. But she came close to me, hugged me, kissed both of my cheeks, and then tried to kiss me on the mouth. When I turned away, she finally turned me loose and headed out of the room.

I was terrified. I waited a while for her to move on down the hallway, and then I got out of my room. I went to the nurses' station to report what had happened, and they reassured me the psychotic woman would be locked up. Shortly thereafter, though, I saw her walking around the nurses' station, the lounge, the cafeteria—wherever she wanted to go. That did it for me. I went to the nurses' station and asked to be transferred to Unit 3. A nursing assistant told me there was also trouble there, so I had to stay here. I knew he was just saying that; I was furious. As I started to walk down the hall, the staff told me the woman would be locked up, but I didn't believe them anymore.

I was scared. Very scared. All I could picture was waking up with her in my room. I got to my room and closed the door. I stared at my big chair; it seemed strong enough to block the door shut. I came up with a plan: I would leave the lights on all night and sit in the lounge chair pressed against the door and put the desk chair in between the desk and the lounge chair. It almost kept the door shut.

I thought about the nursing assistant who checked on us every fifteen minutes. But I just couldn't focus on that; my security was more important. The room checker came around and wasn't happy when he tried to open my door. He started to yell that I couldn't do that. Soon the nurse came down the hall, yelling at me to open the door because I had created a fire hazard. I said no, because I didn't want the psychotic woman to get in my room again.

The nurse warned me that I had three seconds to open the door. Then she yelled out, "One, two, three!" When I still didn't open the door, she said she was going to get someone to take the door down, and she left.

I listened at the door for a while, wondering if they really were going to take the door down. It was quiet for some time, so I started believing they probably weren't going to do anything. I was getting very sleepy, so I rested my head on the pillow on the arm of the chair and fell asleep.

Eventually, after the nurses' shift change, another nurse tapped on my door—softly, but I still jumped. The nurse told me her name and said she had my medications and didn't want me to miss them. I said, "You probably have someone else out there with you." She said she didn't; it was just her. She asked me to open the door just enough for her to get her arm through it with the pills. I did what she said and took the pills. She pulled her arm out again and said she'd be back at 8:00 p.m. to give me the rest of my meds.

She did as she said, and I had my 8:00 p.m. meds. Before she left, she quietly said that I shouldn't keep these chairs blocking the doorway. I didn't respond. I stayed in the chair maybe another half hour; then, since I was so tired, I started thinking about what she had said. I felt a strong urge to lie down on the bed, but I still wanted some protection, so I left the chairs where they were. I figured a small person would be able to get through the door, but not the psychotic woman.

I went to bed and fell asleep immediately.

Monday, August 4, 2014

I awoke to a knock on the door, telling me breakfast was here. I got up, moved the chairs, used the bathroom, and headed for breakfast. After I finished eating, I saw the psychotic woman standing next to the nurses' station. I quickly got my vitals checked and went to get my meds. The nurse told me that if I saw Dr. John before she did, I was to tell him the nurse wanted to talk to him first.

During this morning's group session, we spent the hour talking about coping methods. They gave us a list that might be helpful back at home. Hopefully, I will use some of the suggestions. As the session ended, I saw Dr. John heading toward me. I let him know the nurse wanted to talk with him first, so he headed that way. I waited nearby, and when he came out, we started our session.

He wanted to know what was going on. I explained all that had happened yesterday, and he acknowledged that would have been scary. He told me he would get me moved to Unit 3, which made me so happy. He said he'd see me tomorrow and left.

Thank you, Dr. John, I thought. This nightmare was finally going to end. I skipped the next group session to gather my stuff. As scheduled, a staff person brought in a cart, and we went to Unit 3. I just kept thanking Dr. John over and over in my thoughts.

As I entered Unit 3, all I could think about was that the psychotic woman wasn't there. I was relaxing already, but the fear didn't leave me that fast. Tonight I mostly stayed in my room, trying to calm myself. I was still a little revved up when I went to bed, as I was thinking about the previous night.

I can't believe all that has happened in these past two days.

Tuesday, August 5, 2014

I got up for breakfast and went to the nurses' station for my meds. It was wonderful to see that my daytime nurse was Linda, whom I had previously had as a nurse. I was happy to see her again. We had spent many hours talking during my previous inpatient stays. Our talks were always good, but I didn't always want to agree to what she was telling me. I probably still wouldn't always agree, but she always talked with sincerity.

Unit 3 seemed like the friendlier unit to me. I went to the first group session and, as usual, I had to complete the "daily planning sheet" again. The next session was a spirituality session led by the hospital chaplain. I had heard and talked with him before, and the timing couldn't have been better. He was such a good speaker, and his demeanor was slow and soft, just what I needed. He talked about using all methods available—mental and physical—to move forward in dealing with our issues.

Just as the session finished, Dr. John arrived. He asked how I was doing today and if I felt safe. I said I was starting to feel better, and I definitely felt safer. Thoughts of what had happened the previous couple of days, however, still whirled in my head, making me uneasy. Sadly, my original thoughts of sadness, anxiety, depression, and suicide were creeping back again, even stronger this time. Dr. John reminded me he would be back tomorrow, and then he left.

I sat and thought for a while. I had heard a lot of good advice, but my thoughts always returned to wanting to be with God—and Bill—in Heaven. Those continuous thoughts caused me to be confused by the choices I had left. I wanted Bill; I couldn't have Bill. I seemed to be missing him more all the time, and I didn't know what to do about it. He was the one true love for me on this earth, and I wanted to be reunited with him in Heaven. This life felt like being in a jail.

I remember my mom when she was in the beginning stages of Alzheimer's, saying those same types of words when she no longer could do all she wanted to do. She said being at home felt like being in jail. She had lost my dad years earlier, and life was very confusing. She talked with God often, possibly with some of the same requests I now had.

Thank goodness our next group was going to go for a walk around the healing garden. I walked a few laps before the heat got to me. I sat down in the shade, thinking how crazy the last few days had been, feeling upset that more of the staff hadn't helped me. I was also angry that so much time had been lost because of another patient.

But I needed to relax now and appreciate that Dr. John got me switched to Unit 3. Talking with Dr. John, the chaplain, and Linda (the nurse) and being outside in the garden were calming me. I would try to settle down and start again.

The day ended nicely with a visit from David and Sharon. They brought Uno cards again, which they knew I enjoyed. And it was great to see familiar faces—it reminded me that I was only going to be here for a while. Then it would be back to my own life.

Whatever that is.

Wednesday, August 6, 2014

I was awakened for breakfast, realizing again that I hadn't heard the intercom blasting me awake in the morning. It had to be broken. I noticed I had a lot of anxiety this morning—something to let Dr. John know.

After breakfast, as the staff was taking my vitals, I noticed it was high—around 150/95. I think I was still thinking about my trouble in the other unit. I was hoping my BP would go back down soon, before they told me to see my primary doctor.

Dr. John showed up early today, fortunately. My anxiety wasn't lessening, so, after some thought, Dr. John said he might increase the dosage on one of my meds. He also asked which aftercare I would prefer. That had me guessing that he might be thinking about discharging me in a few days. But it's not good to try to guess. It could have meant he was planning ahead.

The next group session was again a walk in the garden. The weather outside was gorgeous, so I'm sure the staff also wanted to enjoy it. I'm sure they know the garden is calming to us. I walked a little, and then sat in the shade again. The breeze was so nice to feel. Then it was time to go in for lunch.

After lunch, I got my meds and then joined the 1:00 p.m. group. I haven't been getting too much out of this group. Whenever the subject is about using uplifting ideas, it just seems to make me sadder. To me, happiness can't happen until I'm with Bill. Maybe once I get home and experience a couple of these ideas, I might feel a little better. Everyone tells me to perk up, that Bill would want that. I know he would also. Maybe the trick is to start with one new thing and give it a try. I've done that before with various results.

Anyway, that group ended, and after a break it was time for the 3:00 afternoon group. I was leery to go because of the previous session, but I was trying hard not to skip any groups. And luckily, we were just going to draw pictures. This was nice because we were free to keep silent or talk with the other patients. I was starting to be friends with a couple of my fellow patients.

After the session was over, the evening seemed to last forever. I waited for my 9:15 p.m. pills, and I was in bed by 9:25 p.m.

Thursday, August 7, 2014

My normal day…

1. Bathroom

2. Shower

3. Breakfast

4. Vitals

5. Medications

6. Dr. John visit

7. 9:30 a.m. group session

8. 10:30 a.m. group—the garden

9. Lunch

10. Medications

11. Nurse or therapy visit to talk with me

12. 1:00 p.m. group session

13. Break/nap

14. 3:00 p.m. group session

15. Dinner

16. Medications

17. Optional group activity

18. Reading

19. Medications

20. Bed

Friday, August 8, 2014

See my list.

Dr. John came for his daily visit. He let me know I wasn't going to be released today. He would be here Saturday, and he would decide if I was going to be released Monday or Tuesday.

I'm not looking forward to the weekend. They always seem to last so long. At least I've been making a couple of friends.

I was kind of hoping to be released today. I'm starting to miss Lady so much.

Saturday, August 9, 2014

See my previous list.

Dr. John was here as promised for his visit. He talked quite a lot—probably because it's Saturday. I enjoy listening to him; he's always so calming to me.

Robin came to visit me today too. But she has become more than just Father Pat's wife. She's my friend. We bonded the first time we met. It was refreshing to talk with her today.

Sunday, August 10, 2014

See my list.

Monday, August 11, 2014

News from Dr. John. Yes, I am going to be discharged today. He also told me he didn't want me to join any of the aftercare groups. He feels that it's better for me to get back to my outpatient care. I am glad for that.

I just keep thinking about Lady. I want to see her, and I'm sure she wants to see me as well. I just need to pack my things and give Tommy a call to come pick me up. Wow, I'll be back in my own bed again by tonight.

Roger has been watching Lady while I was in the hospital, so after Tommy picked me up, we headed to Roger's house. I was thrilled to see Lady and vice versa. And it was great to see Roger too.

Tommy drove me home and did a few things to help me settle in; then he needed to get home. That was fine, since I just wanted to sit in my living room chair, turn on the TV, and try to relax while petting Lady. It was a big adjustment being home after sixteen days in the hospital. I had started to feel like I was going to live there forever. Parts of that I liked, but parts I definitely didn't.

Tuesday, August 12, 2014

Diana was on vacation today, so this first full day back at home was open for me. And since she was gone, there also would be no group session on Thursday. Good—I could use a break this week.

I was very lazy today, but I did do my shoulder exercises. I tried to do some in the hospital, but it was difficult. My shoulder was starting to hurt more and it was stiffer. So now I really need to get back on track with it.

Tommy had worked in the yard while I was in the hospital, so I had to get outside and take a look. Yes, he was working on some projects; that was good. But of course now I'm thinking about additional projects.

I didn't last very long outside because I still felt as tired as I had before I went into the hospital. And I was saddened that my tiredness was still hanging in there. I decided to just stay in the house and figure out what to have for supper. Nobody was going to bring me my meals anymore.

Wednesday, August 13, 2014

My appointment with Dr. John was very emotional. I am having difficulty with leaving the psych hospital and dealing with the loneliness of being home by myself (besides Lady, my little life saver). I had built up a lot of tension, and it came out, as usual, in sobbing tears. Dr. John decided he wants to see me tomorrow as well, to make sure I'm okay. He's such a caring individual.

Tommy hasn't been able to work for me in over a week because, luckily, the larger downstairs rental came open in the building where Tommy and Melissa rent the smaller upstairs rental with their three children. They've been having difficulty with so little space. But that means Tommy has a lot of work ahead of him—cleaning both apartments, moving all of their belongings, and doing everything else that goes with a move. He's also enrolling all three kids in the fall session of grade school.

I guess I won't see him working at my house for a couple of weeks. And I have such a long list for him already, including trying to wrap up the outside projects before the fall weather gets too cold. Besides that, he's such nice company, and he brings his dog, Bell, to visit with Lady. They like each other.

Thursday, August 14, 2014

My second visit with Dr. John. It's extremely unusual to see him two days in a row, but I was very upset yesterday. Today I'm slightly calmer, although I'm feeling a tremendous amount of tension and anxiety. He's going to leave me on the same meds until we see how I'm doing next week.

Friday, August 15, 2014

Today was the first time I'd seen Ken in weeks. It was good to talk with him again. I started to tell him what was going on while I was in the psych hospital. While he was talking, I could feel my tension rising, and I started having difficulty breathing. This was the beginning of an anxiety attack. Then the tears came. I wasn't able to talk anymore, but I did calm down before our session was over. I guess he got to see my anxiety firsthand.

Saturday, August 16, and Sunday, August 17, 2014

It was a very quiet weekend. Quite lonely. I couldn't get myself to church on Sunday. I felt too much tension and tiredness, so I didn't go. I feel bad about missing church.

Monday, August 18, 2014

Today was an unusually nice day. Dave stopped to see me, and he was the same old Dave—funny one minute and serious the next. It was nice seeing him after so long. And he gave me one of his fabulous hugs. I also wanted to give him one of my books. He was the first one to thoroughly read it for editing.

And in the afternoon, I met up with Rosemary for dinner. We hadn't got together for some time, so our conversation was endless. Rosemary has a good ear and wise comments, which makes her a great one-on-one conversational partner.

Tuesday, August 19, 2014

This morning I saw Megan for my physical therapy for my shoulder. She told me I have only a couple of weeks left in therapy; after that, I'll need to exercise at home. That scares me a little. I know I'm doing well, but I prefer having my exercise in a session when I have to do all the exercises. I've been slowing down my pace at home, but I know I have to keep working on it.

The temperature is nice outside, with no rain, so I'm going to take Lady outside with me and pull weeds. I could spend weeks pulling them and I still wouldn't be finished.

Wednesday, August 20, 2014

In my session with Dr. John today, I was still feeling quite tense. I told him about my anxiety attack in my session with Ken. He seemed surprised by that, but he still wanted to wait until next week on any med changes.

Thursday, August 21, 2014

It's amazing—I don't have any sessions today. I'm going to get back outside to pull more of those weeds. I think they're multiplying. Each day there seems to be more of them. I'm definitely going to use a weed-and-feed product next year.

Friday, August 22, 2014

I saw Ken in the morning, and this time I was calmer. No anxiety attacks today. But I told him the tension is still there. We talked a while about finding the middle ground again.

This evening Beth and I were going to see a movie, but when she checked the schedule, she found that the movie wasn't playing anymore. We decided instead to go shopping and then have dinner.

We went to Kohl's, always a standard with us. I needed to buy some new bras since I had gained weight, and Beth was the perfect person to help me. She found some selections for me and brought them to my dressing room. One after another was no good, but Beth kept finding more for me to choose from. She was also having fun with me, because I was having a problem fitting my new, larger size. She has always been healthier than me. When we were kids, she was jealous of how I could pick out just about anything and it would fit, so I took her verbal abuse and let her get the last laugh.

Finally, the perfect fit. I bought three to last me forever, and we headed out to a Mexican restaurant for yummy strawberry margaritas and dinner. It was nice getting together like this.

Saturday, August 23, 2014

Today was different. No one was around, so I sat alone, deep in my depression, for quite a while. I finally got myself motivated to continue my weed pulling. At least Lady seemed to be enjoying it.

Sunday, August 24, 2014

I went to church in the morning; then I went on my first widows' group outing. One of the ladies lives in a condo village, and they have a building that has a small theater in it. One woman brought some DVDs, and there were three movies for us to pick from. Of course I don't remember the name of the movie we chose, but it was a good one.

I enjoyed some nice conversations with the other widows in the group. I'm becoming closer to a woman called Loralee. We drove together so we could get to know each other better, and it was quite pleasant. This was a pretty good day.

Monday, August 26, 2014

This was going to be a busy day. I had all my sessions including rehab. I need to work hard on my PT since I lost so much time in the hospital.

Wednesday, August 27, 2014

In my session with Dr. John, I told him I was tired of having constant anxiety, so I started drinking a little again. And then the tears came. He reminded me why I shouldn't drink, but I told him it gives me a certain amount of numbness that blocks—for a short time—some of the anxiety. He knew this from previous discussions.

I admitted to him that when I drink I get very depressed and entertain thoughts of suicide. He understood how difficult all of this is, but at the same time he encouraged me to try not to drink. I told him I'd do the best I could.

Thursday, August 28, 2014

Today was my last physical therapy appointment with Megan. I felt sad, and Megan said she was going to miss me. Now I'm on my own.

Friday, August 29, 2014

I had my session with Ken and told him the same things I had told Dr. John—that I was drinking some and feeling extremely depressed. We talked about it and, as usual, I cried.

It was another day of great weather, so when I got home I once again took Lady outside and started pulling weeds. The problem with pulling weeds is that your mind can think about so many things. I kept thinking about Bill, so I felt very depressed.

I know I should try to think about the Father and Jesus and try to listen to them. But when I'm feeling so depressed, I usually cry out for what I want, not what the Father and Jesus necessarily want. Sometimes it feels like a vicious cycle, and I know I will lose if I keep demanding that things go my way.

Saturday, August 30, 2014

Alone… and thinking about Mom's birthday. I wish I could hear some words from her. She's been gone seven years now, and I miss her so.

Sunday, August 31, 2014

After church I spent the day by myself. No pulling weeds, no projects, just alone.

Monday, September 1, 2014 — Rosemary to the rescue

Rosemary called me last night to see how I was doing. When she heard what a rough time I was having, she made plans for us to get together for lunch today. I was pleasantly surprised to have a meal and a great conversation with Rosemary. We parted with a big hug.

Tuesday, September 2, 2014

Robin and I met this morning for coffee and a return to our book club for the two of us. We are reading a book titled *Depression* that uses scripture to discuss the author's ideas on depression. It's quite good, and I'm finding many areas that relate to me.

Wednesday, September 3, 2014

Bible study is back after our August hiatus, and I'm glad. I was missing the interaction all month. It was good to concentrate on the Bible again.

In the afternoon, during my session with Dr. John, I explained that I'm still having a lot of anxiety, but I've had very little to drink. He said he still wants to see how I do for another week.

Thursday, September 4, 2014

No sessions today. Good! Tommy has been accomplishing a lot of work outside, and I wanted to continue my weeding. Cool weather is approaching, so I want to get as much done as possible. My biggest problem is getting tired too quickly. Early on, my therapist warned me that I'd be tired after my therapy was done, and she was right on the dot. After I work for a half hour or so, I need to go in the house and rest for a while. This is discouraging to me because everything is taking so long.

Friday, September 5, 2014

As soon as I was done with my session with Ken, I headed home for more weeding. The days have been cool, but at least they've been clear. This is important because I've been spending most of my weeding time sitting on the ground. I'm trying to work section by section so I don't have to move around too often.

Saturday, September 6, 2014

This morning was the monthly widows' group meeting. I enjoy these meetings, but this morning I was feeling particularly anxious again. As soon as I walked into the room and saw the ladies, I started crying. I wasn't even sure why I was crying. But Rosemary soon saw me and came to my side. That calmed me down enough to stop crying, so I was able to take a seat. Soon Loralee saw me and sat down next to me. I didn't get to talk with her very much, but now that I knew her face, I would watch for her at meetings. Seems she was doing the same thing.

Another familiar face was Laura. She and some others were at another table, so the two of us moved to their table. Now I was feeling more comfortable. The speaker was well liked by the group, but I was more interested in the conversation at the table. Here were women like me, who had lost their husbands.

Their stories were all different, their grief was all different, but we shared the fact that it had happened to us. Any one of us might be smiling one minute and crying the next.

I left, feeling glad I had come. But by the time I drove home, I was already feeling lonely. I tried to do some weeding in the back yard, but my heart just wasn't in it. And, luckily, we had some rain showers later, so I was glad to be inside. But I still managed to hang on to that lonely feeling for the rest of the afternoon and evening.

Sunday, September 7, 2014—Our last day at St. Mark's

Our church has been renting space for mass at St. Mark's for two years now. But they sold the church to another group, so we had to find another rental home. We found a church that has space at 11:30 a.m., so we rented it and will be meeting there after today. Soon, though, we are hoping to find our own meeting place. Even though we changed our church's name to Holy Cross Anglican Church, the term "vagabond church" has been popping up in our parish's conversations.

Once Mass was over, I said hello to a couple of people. When I began to feel a little weepy and tense, I knew it was time to leave.

I got home and again felt lonely and continued to feel tense. This was becoming too common at this intensity lately.

Monday, September 8, 2014

Diana was back today, and we spent most of the session catching up on these last few weeks. I explained to her how emotional I've been lately, and how sick I am of the tension and anxiety I feel all the time. Sometimes I isolate myself, which leaves me feeling lonelier, and sometimes I try to make plans with others, which leaves me feeling more anxious.

"There is no solution," I told her. And then in DPT style, Diana analyzed my thoughts and explained that there is always a solution, a choice, a diversion.

Tell that to another widow.

Tuesday, September 9, 2014

Tuesday has become the official morning for Robin and me to review, over coffee, our book on depression. I enjoy this weekly time when we can talk. Some mornings we'll be talking so much that one of us will have to tell the other that we'd better get started on the book.

On the way home it was raining, so again, there was no good time for weeding. I did have a lot to do in the house, but I felt lazy again. This laziness is becoming a bad habit. Thank goodness Tommy is helping me out.

Thursday, September 11, 2014

When I called Roger this afternoon, he told me Serena, his fourteen-year-old yellow Labrador, isn't doing well. It's an ongoing thing—she hasn't been eating regularly and she's been having a lot of trouble walking. And she's sleeping most of the time. He's been thinking about taking her to the veterinarian again. He's very worried about her, and now, so am I. I've been very close to his dogs; they mean a lot to me.

Tonight was Bible study. We finished eating and had just started the study when the phone rang. It was Roger, telling me the sad news that his dog Serena had just died. I screamed, "Oh no!" so I had the whole group worrying about me. Roger explained that she had been lying on the kitchen floor, and he noticed fluids around her mouth. He went to her but instantly knew she felt wrong.

We just sat on the phone, crying. She was such a sweet dog—it was a terribly sad moment. I also thought about Lady. She's only one year younger than Serena and also has developed problems with her legs and isn't always interested in eating. Now I'm fearing the worst. I don't know how I would continue to exist without Lady. The house would genuinely be empty with just me. After all the years of so much activity in our house, it would be empty.

Friday, September 12, 2014

I had my session with Ken today. I told him I was struggling this past week and that I was really affected by the death of Roger's dog. We talked about that for a while. And as he had been saying in the past, I need to have outside contacts to keep my mind off things. He calls it a middle ground for me. He doesn't expect that I'll reach the highest point, but he wants to pull me out of the deepest point that I so often am in.

I left a little lighter. But when I got home there was no sign of Tommy, so I called him. He isn't feeling well so he isn't coming over today. I understand, but I'm disappointed. I already felt lonely, and he usually perks me up a little.

I started watching TV and drifted into a lazy afternoon. It feels like the wind has been knocked out of me.

I got together with Beth this morning—it's been about a month since we were able to do anything. We did a little rummaging, and then we went back to my house. I had recently bought an outside wood burner, and she volunteered to put it together for me. She was pretty fast about it too. Then she had to head home. It was a nice time of visiting with her.

In the late afternoon I had to get ready for the church's annual Holy Cross Anglican Church banquet. A CANA bishop would be joining us to give us a short talk, and he would also be with us at mass tomorrow—the first day our vagabond church will go to our new temporary home. We also hired a real estate broker and formed a committee to increase our chances of finding a building we can buy.

I was rushing to get my promised centerpieces with flowers from my yard done. Of course it took longer than expected, which was okay, since I started early just in case. Looking at the centerpieces, I realized I would have trouble bringing all five in my car. Not to mention it would wear me out going back and forth to load them. I called Robin, and she sent two of her children to help. That was great, because then I only had to bring one, and in addition, candles and holders, and silverware. That was enough of a load.

Fr. Pat's brother, a chef, did the cooking, so we had a wonderfully executed gourmet meal. It was delicious, and it seemed like everyone had a great time.

Sunday, September 14, 2014

For our first time using this building, the mass was wonderfully done and the church building looks like it will be a good temporary home.

Once I got home, I sat down in a lounge chair and fell asleep. I guess I wasn't able to handle a late night followed by an early morning of activity.

Monday, September 15, 2014

Today was a rainy day, and my body felt the dampness. I got up early because today was my last appointment with my shoulder surgeon. I felt so tired again that I decided to rest until I had to leave.

I fell asleep and woke up two hours later, with only fifteen minutes to get to my appointment. I put myself in high gear and made it to the doctor's office on time. But as I was walking back to my car, I felt that same weariness. I got home and gave in to my lounge chair. This time I didn't sleep, but it took me a while to rest before I was up to doing much of anything.

I felt very tense as evening approached, with thoughts of Bill swirling in my head. I made myself a drink, knowing Dr. John wouldn't approve, but drinking still calms me down a little. I finished my drink, took care of Lady, and went to bed.

Tuesday, September 16, 2014

I met Robin at a restaurant for our two-person book club. It was quite a nice break for me, sipping coffee and having time to chat with Robin. I'm so glad she suggested it.

Wednesday, September 17, 2014

Bible study morning. But before that, a repairman came to look at my living room fan. Tommy had taken it apart and talked with the repairman, but Tommy and his three kids had come down with the flu, so I was all alone with this man as we stared up at the ceiling. He said it would've been better if it hadn't been taken apart. Now Tommy would have to remove the fan from the ceiling and take it to the repair shop.

Shortly after, the Bible study group arrived. It was another interesting time having Fr. Pat decipher the scriptures for us.

Later was my appointment with Dr. John. I let him know I was still feeling quite depressed and was still crying quite a bit. And, yes, I told him I was still using alcohol to block these feelings. He asked what time of day was the hardest for me, and I said the evenings were when I felt the most anxious, and that's when I would take a drink or two. He suggested moving the times I take one of my anti-anxiety meds to later in the day to decrease my anxiety, hoping to relieve the desire for the numbness that alcohol brings. I agreed to try that.

Thursday, September 18, 2014

The day started with my 1:00 p.m. DPT group session. This still isn't my favorite session, but I never seem to like being in a group. I much prefer the one-on-one time. I felt like crying during most of the session, so I didn't participate at all. I was doing everything to hold back the tears and left feeling miserable.

Tonight is Bible study, and this time we're going to meet at Helena's house. Helena is now a member of the church, and she and her mother, Ester, wanted to come to the Thursday night sessions, but Esther is extremely allergic to dogs so they would never be able to come to my house. So we worked out a deal: Esther stays with Helena one month, and the alternate month with her son. So from now on, during the month that Esther is with Helena, we will have Thursday night Bible study at their house. On the opposite months, we'll be at my house. I'm glad we found a solution.

Friday, September 19, 2014

In my session with Ken today, I told him about Dr. John's suggestion to take my anti-anxiety pills later to curb my desire to drink in the evening due to anxiety. I explained to Ken that I tried it, and it isn't working. In fact, I'm anxious all day long now. He reminded me to talk with Dr. John, and that is my plan.

As I was listening to him talk, I started feeling more and more anxious. I had to stop him and tell him I was going into my second anxiety attack. Soon I was crying quite hard, and I told him that this has been happening more and more. He told me to talk with Dr. John about this too; maybe he could adjust or add a medication to help me.

Saturday, September 20, 2014

This morning I met with Beth for a while. We did some rummaging and had lunch together. It was a shorter visit since we both had plans later, but at least we got together.

Later in the afternoon was my granddaughter Jessica's birthday party. They have fixed up their back yard with a deck and a tiki bar, which worked really well for the party. My in-laws, Scott, Deb, and Stephanie, and Julie, Bob, and William were there, amongst other people I didn't know.

I was doing okay at first, but as the evening approached and the party lights went on, I could hear the party was getting nosier, and my relatives were moving around to visit with other people. I felt awkward, just sitting in a chair and not talking to anyone. Soon I was feeling lonely and anxious too, and I started crying—thank goodness it was dark by this time.

I wanted to leave, but I had come with Scott, Deb, and Stephanie. When I had a chance, I went over to talk to Deb. Before I could say anything, she said we were leaving soon.

I felt so sad when I got home. I knew I couldn't go straight to bed, so I watched TV for a while. When I realized I was going to have a hard time waking up for church the next day, I tried to get to sleep.

Sunday, September 21, 2014

I was right. I was still half asleep as I turned off my alarm when it buzzed. I thought I was just turning off the warning buzzer, but no, I turned off the whole thing. I woke up later, too late to get to church. Very embarrassing.

The rest of the day proved rainy and lonely—not to mention the anxiety I can't shake. It was a long day. I was glad to have some activity coming up the next few days.

Monday, September 22, 2014

This time, Robin, Rosemary, and I joined forces and had coffee together. I wondered how it would turn out—and I was delighted. We all enjoyed each other and had enough talk to last longer if we would have had the time. We agreed to meet every two or three months.

I did get some weeding done this afternoon. Not a lot, as usual, but I convinced myself that at least I was slowly finishing a large section. Tommy also worked around the yard. I think I got tired enough to be able to relax during the evening for a change.

Tuesday, September 23, 2014

A busy day today. It started with Robin and me doing our two-person book club. Next was my session with Diana. We had a good talk, although sometimes I feel like she's just reading from the workbook. She has a quick mind, though, and often comes up with questions that surprise me.

The third meeting was quite a surprise—one of the nurses I used to work with called me a few days back. She and another woman I knew wanted to meet me after they got off work. I was shocked, since we hadn't seen each other for a couple of years. I said yes, and then later I headed to the restaurant.

When I arrived, I looked carefully to see if they were already there. I didn't see them, so I was seated outside on a cozy little bridge with a row of tables and chairs. I waited for some time and got thirsty, so I asked for water. Realizing my anxiety was building fast, I ordered a beer too. After it seemed like I'd waited quite a long time, I started wondering whether to go or wait a while longer. Then I heard my name. A fourth nurse that I also knew had showed up and saw me. She said the other two were at the other end of the patio. So finally we were all together and had a nice dinner. It was great seeing them again, and I was glad they had initiated the visit.

But, like clockwork, I got in my car and already felt alone and sad. I used to meet friends after work, but when I headed home—Bill was always there.

Wednesday, September 24, 2014

After Bible study, I left for my appointment with Dr. John. I had waited all week to tell him that pushing the time back in taking my anti-anxiety pill was making it worse. Now I was extremely anxious in the afternoon, and when I started taking my pill, it never quite slowed down the tension.

When I told him this, he looked disappointed. I suggested maybe I could alternate the two pills that I was taking at the same time so that I would be taking a pill more often. He thought that was a good idea—so here we go, starting over again.

Thursday, September 25, 2014

Another busy day. A long time ago, Bill's cousin, Cheryl, called me. I always meant to call her back, but I never did. Finally last week I gave her a call, and she was delighted to hear from me. We made plans to have lunch today.

I was anxious as usual as I walked into the restaurant. It was one Bill and I had eaten at many years ago, so I hoped it would be okay. I waited for a while and secretly wanted to leave because I was getting quite nervous. But she arrived and we got a seat. We had a nice time talking, catching up on some family stuff. It was pleasant getting together with her, and we promised to do it again.

Next was my DPT group session. This week I tried harder to participate since I didn't say anything last week. It worked a little better, and I actually made a few comments.

And lastly, Bible study was at Helene's house. I was relaxing before needing to leave for Helene's when I got a call from Marty. Her husband Terry was working tonight, so she wondered if she could get a ride from me. I told her of course, but as I was hanging up the phone I was thinking about how tired I was and that I hoped I could figure out how to get from Marty's house to Helene's house.

Thanks to my car's mapping system, we got there on time, which amazed me. And I was happy to find out that Helene's son, Max, was going to drive her home. I worry because my eyes haven't been very good lately. Driving in the dark can be especially difficult, more so if I'm tired.

Friday, September 26, 2014

I was a little calmer at my session with Ken today. I told him about the med change Dr. John and I had made, alternating the two anti-anxiety pills starting at noon. He too hoped this would help. We continued our talk on finding a middle ground by finding new things to do. *Does weeding count?* I questioned

In the afternoon I did get in a little weeding, but again I was tired—I think because of my shoulder surgery, and when I'm so depressed it saps the energy right out of me. I went back inside my house and spent another long night alone.

Saturday, September 27, through
Monday, September 29, 2014

Three long, lonely days.

Tuesday, September 30, 2014

I only have my appointment with Diana today. I told her about the med changes. She isn't a fan of most drugs, so she was glad he didn't increase anything. We talked about all sorts of things today.

Wednesday, October 1, 2014

Bible study today. My session with Dr. John was rescheduled to tomorrow. After Bible study was over, I went back outside for more weeding, although I found it was a lot cooler today. It wasn't too bad in the sun, but I quit because I was getting too cold. Tommy trudged on. I showed him which of the large weeds to pull, the ones I didn't have the strength to remove. He did a fabulous job—and he did a lot of it.

Oh, to have his energy! I thought. I remember having that kind of energy in my thirties.

Thursday, October 2, 2014

What an extremely busy day. First I met Loralee (from the widows' group) for coffee. I was a little nervous because we hadn't really talked one-on-one yet. But we had a very nice conversation, mostly about our commonality. We plan on doing it again.

Next I had my DPT group session, which was okay today.

Then I had my appointment with Dr. John. We mostly discussed pills. I told him that alternating the two pills had helped some, but I was still feeling the anxiety. He decided to switch one medication to another with a longer half-life, and added a medication I hadn't been taking since after my surgery, when the hospital took me off everything. He said we would watch for the next couple of weeks to see if this would help.

Next was my Bible study, and it was uplifting and wonderful. But, as usual, after everyone left and my busy day was done, I returned to feeling lonely. It had to be Bill that was there for me afterward, or I was lonely, period.

Friday, October 3, 2014

I had one appointment today with Ken. Considering I wasn't concentrating very well, we had a good talk. But halfway through, I told him about our wedding anniversary coming up in a couple of weeks, and I started crying. He kept trying to talk with me, but my tears were insistent. I left still wiping the tears from my eyes.

Saturday, October 4, 2014

Saturday was a quiet day at home with a chance to meditate on my usual disturbing thoughts. I tried doing some weeding, but that didn't work very well. I was stuck in my living room chair, flipping channels and looking for something that would distract me from feeling the way I did, without much luck.

Sunday, October 5, 2014

Roger and Terry picked up their new yellow Labrador puppy today. I was determined to see the new puppy named Natasha, Tasha for short. Once I saw that puppy, I picked her up and didn't want to let go. I sat on the couch so she would have more room to move around. Happily she wanted to spend a good amount of time with me, and I loved it. What a little furball. And that puppy breath—the best!

Monday, October 6, 2014

No sessions today, so I asked Tommy if we could go to the grocery store. My cupboards were really empty, and I was running out of soda. When we got to the store, I realized I had forgotten my checkbook, and I wanted to deposit a check. Tommy drove home to get it as I continued shopping.

I got to the last row of the store, and it suddenly hit me that my stomach was in a knot and I was approaching a panic attack. I stood still, breathing, and Tommy appeared behind me. I was so relieved that I wanted to hug him. The panicky feeling didn't go away, but it lessened in severity. Still, I wanted to get out of that store as fast as possible.

Tuesday, October 7, 2014

I only had one session today, with Diana. I got quite emotional with her, first telling her about the panic attacks, and next telling her my wedding anniversary was in two weeks. I don't know if she exactly knew what to say about it. I told her it was the most important day in my life. I had never felt such warmth in my heart, especially when I looked into Bill's eyes. The depth of his eyes was enormous. The sincerity and love I saw there were piercing. We knew we were meant to be together, forever.

I left drying my eyes. This afternoon I did yard work with Tommy.

Wednesday, October 8, 2014

It's been a very tense morning. And drowsy—I don't know what that's about.

Today I saw Dr. John. I was hoping he would have the right words to calm me down. I felt like I was going to have a panic attack any moment. He listened intently as I started to explain about my panic attacks that happened three to four times in the past week in front of other people. As usual, I started to cry, trying to explain how I was feeling. I was using my standard phrase, "I can't do this anymore," which can mean so many things.

I heard Dr. John say to himself, "I have to do something to stop this." And then he was prescribing me a new drug. Just a week's worth to see how I'll do with it. We'll see.

Thursday, October 9, 2014

I awoke feeling rushed and tense. I was to meet with Rosemary for coffee, but I was dragging and not in a very good mood. I figured things would look up when I met her. She has a way about her that brightens my day.

As our coffee break started, Rosemary said she knew before I sat down that I was having a hard time. There were a lot of tears during out talk, but she somehow got me into a conversation in which I was talking and talking. I complemented her on getting me to talk casually, and she admitted that was what she was trying to do.

Next I had to get to my DPT group session. That too was a pretty good session. I didn't feel pressured or tense during the session—and that was a good improvement, considering how I felt this morning.

After the session, I went home hoping to do some yard work, but it was still quite chilly outside. Instead I chose to stay inside and do some writing. It was cozier, and the time flies when I write. I have the TV on in the background, and I just heard they are playing the movie *The Ghost and Mrs. Muir*. It's always been one of my favorites, but it has grown in importance because Mrs. Muir waits her whole adult life waiting for her death so she can again meet up with the Ghost. It reminds me of my wait for my death so I can again meet up with Bill.

Friday, October 10, 2013

Ken worked hard in our session to persuade me to find some diversions that will give me more peace. He has mentioned a couple of times that he has started a topic with me and I've gained that sparkle in my eye and am interested in talking about that topic. I can't feel it, but I'm sure he's right. I know there are times—especially in Bible study— that I get fascinated by a topic and the tension and anxiety go away for a while.

Saturday, October 11, 2014

Again, I felt shaky heading to the widows' group meeting. I get nervous just before I have to walk in. It helps when I see someone I know right away. But when I have to search for a friendly face, I get anxious enough to feel like leaving.

I ran into Laura, so I sat down next to her. That helped. The talk began, but I didn't care for it very much. And it was long. I tried to sit quietly, waiting for it to end, but the knot in my stomach turned into a panic attack, until I couldn't sit there anymore. I headed out of the room, with most people probably thinking I was going to the bathroom. I did, but it was to cry and try some deep, slow breathing.

I heard applause, so I knew the talk was over. I wiped my eyes and went back into the room. Rosemary saw me and started talking to me, confirming that I had been troubled. She gave me a hug, and I left.

Sunday, October 12, 2014

I awoke to a drizzly, cool day. I went to church, then afterward I knew my plans to weed were shot. I got home and got inside the house when I heard the rain really coming down. That was it. I was really tired after church, so I sat in my favorite lounge chair and turned on the TV. Putting the TV on would make it easier to take a nap. And as usual, Lady was taking a nap right next to me.

Not much got done today.

Monday, October 13, 2014

Today was even worse. I didn't have any appointments, and Tommy said he couldn't come over today, so I sat in the same chair and fell asleep—although this time I slept one and a half hours. I couldn't believe it when I saw the clock.

I got Lady's food ready, I saw that it was still dreary outside, and I still felt very weak and tired. I watched a couple of TV programs first, but then I fell asleep again. This time I kept waking up, but each time I felt as tired, so I would fall asleep again.

I finally decided to stop this pattern, so I came into my computer room and did some writing. Of course, that meant I was wide awake and ready to spend hours at the computer, but by 11:00 p.m. Lady was standing in front of the bed barking. Since she can't get up on the bed anymore, I felt guilty and closed up the house and helped her into bed. She was asleep in a minute, looking as cute as a little puppy. Then I felt tired again, so I went to bed as well.

Tuesday, October 14, 2014

I started my day with Diana's session. I was tense like last time, but we started talking, and the subject of my wedding anniversary came up. I also mentioned the panic attacks I keep having. She was trying to put me in a better place. She asked what I did when I was in a panic attack. Did I try any of the DPT teachings?

I said I tried to watch my breathing—keeping it slow with deep breaths. She said that was good; at least I was attempting to stop it. She said I need to keep doing this.

Wednesday, October 15, 2014

During Bible study today, Lady was a little stinker. Tommy came without Bell, and Lady didn't seem convinced she wasn't there. So she kept barking and barking. I could stop her for a while, but then she'd start again. I even put her outside in the back yard, but then she started barking at the back door. Needless to say, I missed a lot of the Bible study.

Next was my appointment with Dr. John. He was curious to see if the pill changes had helped me. I told him, "Not since Tuesday. I had another three to four anxiety attacks, the last on Monday. But the last couple of days I seemed to have calmed down a little."

He was pleased and gave me a prescription for another two weeks. And we'll see how I'm doing the next week.

Thursday, October 15, 2014

I went to my DPT group session today. One of the girls brought in bags with heather in them. They smelled so good; most of us were holding them by our noses during the session. It was a decent session, with most of us giving out comments as Diana wrote on the blackboard.

Friday, October 16, 2014

Ken is continuing to talk about diversions in my life. The best I can come up with is having coffee with some of my friends, and he feels that is very important.

Saturday, October 17, 2014

Beth is busy this morning, so I'm hoping the drizzle goes away so I can do a few things outside.

In the mid-afternoon, I'm invited to Helena's house for a goodbye to her son as he enters the Marines. He is such a brave soul. I will pray for him and all the other soldiers.

Sunday, October 18, 2014

After church I headed home, not feeling very well. I was exhausted and weak. It was such a beautiful day that I desperately wanted to work outside, but I didn't have the energy for it. So, reluctantly, I sat down in a chair in the living room and took a nap.

What a waste of a beautiful day.

Monday, October 19, 2014

I still wasn't feeling well today, but Tommy and I were supposed to go to Roger's house so Tommy could cut wood and I could play with Roger's six-week-old puppy. She's a doll, but she has a lot of little sharp teeth and nails. I still had a great time playing with her.

I got home and had a call from Billy. He, Heidi, and Emily are in town during their move back to Wisconsin, so Julie and Bob asked us over for a get-together and pizza. It was a nice evening until I couldn't find my purse. We looked everywhere, deciding I had put it on my trunk when I was helping Lady get into the car. I was sure it was lost in the street, and probably stolen. I called the police and gave them all the information.

With that problem on my mind, I had trouble falling to sleep tonight.

Tuesday, October 20, 2014

After I cancelled all my credit cards in the morning, I got a call from Julie saying they had found my purse in their driveway. I was so happy. Cancelling the charge cards was difficult and time-consuming, but nothing compared to having to redo my checkbook, insurance cards, and license. I was thrilled that the crisis was over.

I was quite teary-eyed when I went to my session with Diana. First I told her what had happened, but then I returned to my story about facing our marriage anniversary Sunday and how affected I was about it. I cried through much of the session. Diana is trying very hard to get me to think about other things, but with no luck so far.

Wednesday, October 21, 2014

We had Bible study this morning. I was feeling emotional, but I think I hid it well. The study itself went well, and it was good being with that group. They always make me feel better. As usual, Tommy stayed afterward to work at my house today.

Later this afternoon I had an appointment with Dr. John. There I completely fell apart. I told him I didn't want to live past Sunday and blurted out a lot of things like *not wanting to do this anymore* and *I can't live this way*. I knew our wedding anniversary was bringing up a lot of these feelings. But it's true—it's been over five years that I've been suffering like this, and it takes so much out of me that I just want to end this life and go to Heaven. I just don't know if doing what I want will get me to Heaven.

Thursday, October 22, 2014

This morning I got up a little earlier and did some yard work for a change. I had until 12:45 p.m. to leave before my DPT group session began.

Thursday night is Bible study night, which is always good. Afterward, Father stayed for a little while to talk to me about things that are bothering me. I also wanted confession. And…I wanted to ask Father if it was okay for me to come up when he asks for birthdays or anniversaries, and if I could bring up a picture of Bill and me getting married. He gave me a blessing.

Friday, October 23, 2014

Ken was my only session today. I can tell his style is trying to bring up all kinds of subjects and see if I get interested in any of them. Some I do, and it works, but some I don't—and those can make me even sadder.

Saturday, October 24, 2014

Beth came over so we could do some rummaging and shopping today. We went to quite a few places, so my legs were really worn out. Afterward we had a simple but nice Mexican meal.

By the time we got home, Tommy was working at my house. He hadn't been able to work Thursday or Friday, so he asked if he could work today. It was fine with me.

I started the day in church, with the special blessing from Fr. Pat. But when church was done, I really wanted to get home. I wanted to be alone with Bill today. Thoughts of our marriage anniversary brought me to thoughts of our whole life together.

I can't begin to describe the love we had for one another. We existed for one another. One touch brought immense joy to us. A hug, holding hands, a kiss. Words were seldom needed, but we managed to have plenty of those also. But much more thought than that is unbearable. I prefer to be numb. It's more comforting.

Another thing we had in common was God. We always knew God loved us, and Bill was immensely involved in church. I could see the devotion in his mannerisms during church, and he loved church hymns. I didn't show it as much in my roles in church, but I still had the faith, the hope, and the trust.

And most of all, as much as Bill and I loved one another, we knew there was no doubt that there was a Higher Being: God the Father, God the Son, and God the Holy Spirit. He was always a part of our lives, from going to church, to prayers, to how we decorated our house. We loved crucifixes and had them in almost every room. Now I have added plaques showing quotes from the Bible and key words such as Faith, Hope, and Trust. That way, as I walk through my house I'm constantly reminded what God has done for me, and what I should be doing for God.

Until the day I die, I will sorrowfully miss Bill.

Summary

Where do I go from here? I wonder. I am solid in my belief in God, and it is growing now that I am concentrating on the Bible so much. And I am trying to listen to God—His will— more than just asking God for endless requests. I continue to go to church and Bible study. I listen as carefully as I possibly can and try to understand all I can.

I have no doubt in my mind that God loves me and hopes for me to join him in Heaven someday. My problem is that I don't have the patience to wait. I'm stuck. The cross tells us that life won't always be easy, but I find that hard to bear. Even momentary times of joy leave me quickly. I can look at a flower in my garden, smile for a moment, and return to my grief the next second, not wanting to be in the garden anymore because I used to enjoy it with Bill.

When my thoughts become too negative, I suspect that the devil is trying to get close to me. And at times like those, I am the most vulnerable. I want the devil to stay away from me and my thoughts. Quite often, when my mind drifts toward suicide or other horrible thoughts, I'll shout, "In the name of God; devil, leave me and my house!"

It's amazing how well that works. God's help protects my life.

I have this large hole in my heart since Bill has been gone. I'm not sure where he is. Is he sleeping? Is he with me? Is he busy with his new life in Heaven? I have so many questions.

I've sadly read in scriptures that there is no marriage in Heaven, but I don't want him to be one of a trillion people that I occasionally see and say hello to. At the least, I want to continue to be his partner, to feel our love—for eternity. To be able to pray together, be in awe of Jesus together, work together. Whatever we do in heaven, I want to do it together with Bill—for eternity.

But none of us in this life knows what it's like to be in Heaven. We can't understand God's plan until we get there.

I have another larger hole in my heart. This one only God can fill. He, in Three, is the most powerful source of love I have. My focus since Bill has been gone is my relationship with God. But I want it to include Bill. In the Bible, God says we should be similar to Him. Because he is perfect, we should try to be perfect. I want to be as close to this as I can. I'm sure Bill already is. I can picture Bill holding his drill, asking God if there is anything he can do for him.

One of my favorite non-religious memorial poems is this:

> *You are not forgotten loved one*
> *Nor will you ever be*
> *As long as life and memory last*
> *We will remember thee.*

Even in my impatient mind, I have a favorite Psalm:

> *Blessed be the LORD, for he has heard the sound of my*
> *pleading. The LORD is my strength and my shield,*
> *In him my heart trusts, and I find help; then my heart exults,*
> *and with my song I give him thanks. (Psalm 27:6–7)*

THE END

About the Author

JEAN KAISERLING is a Wisconsin resident who knows how to deal with cold winters—she spends a great deal of time enjoying her home's lush, perennial gardens in the springtime of the year. She takes comfort in a close relationship with God, as she talks with Him daily; but more importantly, she *listens* to Him.

The idea for Jean's first book, ***I Know You Love Me: To My Husband, Bill*** came quickly, as she began writing journal entries about losing her husband, Bill. Then, she realized the details were something more than just journal entries—they were a journey—through the life and love she shared with Bill.

And continuing on in the journey, Jean's next memoir, ***The Inpatient Years***, takes readers through her everyday life and through the ups and downs of the healing process.

Jean hopes her journey through the Valley of the Shadow of Death will comfort others.